Dedicated to my loving wife Amanda.
Without her, this book would have always been halfway done.

Debt Free Mind

Table of Contents

Foreword

Why waste your time learning about money? Aren't we raised to know everything we need to know? Didn't Mom and Dad teach us everything? Step one, get a job. Step two, collect a paycheck. Step three, spend that paycheck. Step four, repeat steps two and three until death. This is the financial circle of life. Make money to spend money.

But what if there is more to it? What if there is something between step two and step three that we never learned from our parents?

We get stuck in financial pits, crushed by debt, because we have been convinced that creating wealth is difficult. We assume people who have any kind of wealth must have high paying jobs or were born into it. Therefore, the only way you could ever have wealth is to have a high paying job as well.

FALSE.

There is no secret to wealth.

Let me repeat for emphasis; **there is no secret to wealth.**

There is only patience.

I want you to build wealth. A wealthy society is a healthy society. To accomplish this, I need to teach you two things, patience and awareness. You need patience over your purchases and awareness that everything around you is created to build a sense of urgency. This urgency is an illusion designed by companies to make you feel that if you don't have what they're selling right now, you must be a loser.

Saving money to create wealth does not make you a loser.

There is an easy formula to follow: the more you save and the less you spend, the more money you will have. This is all you need to know in order to build wealth. Teach yourself to save more than you spend. If you make $10, don't spend $10. And certainly don't spend $12.

That's the secret. Now, you can throw your other finance books in the trash.

If only it were that simple. This is the part where patience and awareness come in. I want to build your financial patience by enhancing your awareness of how society convinces you to spend more than you make.

I can hear you saying, "Commercials and society don't influence me. I'm too smart for that." My response would be if you're reading a book about debt, maybe you've been a little more influenced than you think. Hell, I was. I still am a little. It's hard in a society so built around credit to view debt in a negative light. Mom and Dad certainly didn't. It's practically part of our American DNA, evolved over many generations.

It has never been easier to get credit. Only a generation ago, it was **hard** to get a credit card. You had to **apply** and **prove** you knew how to manage your money. Now, you have to prove you have a pulse. America is ranked #2 in the world for how easy it is to obtain credit. Second only to some country even more in debt than us.

If you take one thing away from this book, let it be this: When you finance a purchase, you don't own what you just bought. What you've done is **promise** to buy the item - eventually. Don't believe me? Stop making payments on your car loan. The bank will make it crystal clear who **owns** the car. It ain't you.

The loan could be for $15,000 and you could have paid $14,999 on it. If you do not pay that last dollar, the bank can take the car back. Your $14,999 be damned. Why can they do this? Because the bank owns the car, not you.

What do you call someone who owns nothing and owes a lot of money to other people? Broke. WE'RE ALL BROKE. This is the wake up call.

In college I was fortunate to have access to lots of Magic Money, also known as credit cards. I call them magic because of their ability to grant any wish you have without having to pay anything to get it. At least not at that exact moment.

This Magic Money bought me a lot of great things. It bought me a surround sound system for my dorm room, a motorcycle, and an education. How, you ask, could I afford a motorcycle to impress my girlfriend, a killer sound system, and other such things while, at the same time, taking out loans to pay for college? I couldn't. But nobody told me that. In fact, this type of behavior was, and still is, encouraged.

I maxed out two credit cards with one purchase.

It didn't matter to me; I planned on paying them off eventually. I had no real expenses to speak of. My university fed me for free and I paid them nothing to attend. All I had to do was circle the word "Accept" five or so times and sign my name at the bottom of the page. Sure, there was a bunch of numbers next to the words "Accept," but who cares about them? Isn't this what everyone going to college does?

Fortunately, I figured out early enough that having two maxed out credit cards is absolutely horrible. I would make the minimum payments each month, but my bill never seemed to get any smaller. I started making large, lump sum payments on both cards and was able to pay them off long before I graduated. Had I not, I would have had that credit card debt on top of my student loan debt burden.

Unfortunately, I only figured out what my college loan total was when I graduated and the mail started to roll in. The numbers that had been next to the word "Accept" were $2,500, and I was agreeing to borrow that every semester.

This book is a compilation of what I have learned while digging myself out of the debt hole my college education and poor spending habits put me in. Our parents tried their best to teach us everything we would need to prosper in this world, but these are lessons I had to learn the hard way. It is my hope that these lessons will help you avoid or overcome the same unfortunate situation.

Chapter 1:

Surviving College and Loans

Tip1: College Loans for Drinking

The Diamond
no better re-rack

    College loans are available to pay for classes, books, and resident housing. But how surprising would it be if college loans were used for buying alcohol or bar hopping? Well, surprise, they are.

    This is nothing new. College loans have been used for beer for as long as they have existed. Don't worry, Mom and Dad probably did it too. You may wonder how this is possible, how federal loan money could be used to pay for things like toga parties and cover charges. It's really quite simple. The only catch is you have to get it out of your head that there is a difference between money you borrow and money you earn.

This is something that I have been guilty of for most of my life. Money I borrowed for college was to pay for my classes and for my books. The money I earned, working on campus and off, was my money to spend on whatever I wanted that was not school-related. I worked hard so I could buy a flat screen TV and surround sound system for my dorm room. I worked hard to pay $20 cover charges at bars for the privilege of buying overpriced drinks for my girlfriend. I used my earned money for anything and everything except my college education.

To pay for my college degree, I used borrowed money. This was my "un-fun money" that paid for serious things such as tuition, books, and other classroom supplies. Why would I ever want to spend my earned money on un-fun things when I could use borrowed money for them? This goes against everything the fun-seeking part of our brains tells us to do.

In the real world, there is no division between earned money and borrowed money. The distinction exists only in our minds. When it comes to expenses, how the money made its way into your bank account is irrelevant. At some point it all becomes **spent money**. Spent money doesn't care if you worked hard hours after class to earn your money or if you signed your life away to borrow money.

To frame this in a different way, imagine reversing the roles of earned and borrowed money. With your earned money, you work hard to pay for your tuition, books, and housing. After all of this, you have no money left for any fun activities, so you take out personal loans to go to nightclubs, buy a sweet TV for your dorm, and take awesome spring break vacations.

THIS SOUNDS RIDICULOUS.

But really, there is no difference between this reversed order set-up and the one college students live every day. I know. I lived it. If you earn any money while you are attending college, some, if not most, should be going toward paying your tuition. Otherwise, you are doing nothing more than borrowing money to party.

In my case, I paid nothing toward my tuition. My tuition was covered entirely by loans. I'm not suggesting I should have put everything I earned toward paying my tuition and lived like a monk. That would have made the experience miserable. I'm suggesting I could have supplemented some of my income in place of loans. It certainly would have been better than none.

To leave you with one last example, suppose you lend me $100. The next week we go out to a bar and you watch me blow $150 dollars on food and drinks. When you ask me why I haven't paid you back even though I clearly have the money to spend, my reply is, "This was money Mom and Dad gave me; I told you I'd pay you back out of my next paycheck." Would you care where my money came from? Or only that I had money and used it for a night out instead of paying back my loan from you?

My sentiments exactly - it's all the same money.

Do not let yourself be duped into thinking that it is OK to let yourself rack up college debt simply because it is offered to you. If you can afford to pay something, anything, toward your college education, do it.

Tip 2: College Loans Are Real Money

Such an obvious statement, I know, but I need to say it because of how I and so many others treat their loans. As I went through college I felt no pressure to pay off my loans. To me, loans were a convenience. I was not forced to worry about money and was free to worry about other pressing issues, like how to get this brown-eyed girl named Amanda to date me and where to get the best price on a thirty of Keystone. Sure, Uncle Bob may have suggested that I pay something toward my loans before graduation, but doesn't he always make such outrageous suggestions? His mantra of "At least pay the interest" fell on deaf ears.

My advice: listen to Uncle Bob and pay your loans as you go. Especially if you have unsubsidized loans. Unsubsidized loans have the unfortunate quality of accruing interest while you are still in college. Subsidized loans on the other hand do not accrue interest until your repayment period begins.

To demonstrate the difference, imagine you borrow $4,000 in your freshman year, but then pay for the rest of your education in full (impressive). The chart below shows how much you save with a subsidized loan and why it is important if you have an unsubsidized loan to (at a minimum) pay the interest as it accrues.

College Loans	Subsidized	Unsubsidized	Difference
Loan Value	$4,000	$4,000	
Interest	0%	6%	
Due @Grad	$4,000	$5,081.96	$1,081.96

You have no say in taking either a subsidized or unsubsidized loan. That is a "need-based" decision the government makes after receiving your FAFSA form. Whichever loan structure you have, it is beneficial to make payments towards it before you graduate. It becomes even more vital if you have an unsubsidized loan as the above chart clearly demonstrates. Climbing out of debt is an incredible burden. Paying off some of the loans before they become due gives you a fantastic head start. Paying only $50 a month toward this loan would reduce your obligation at graduation to $2,377. That is much better than $5,000.

I was unable to do this for a couple of reasons. The first being my motorcycle and another being that my dorm room clearly needed a large flat screen TV, dual computer monitors, and a surround sound system. My priorities were a little skewed. Don't let yours be.

Being involved in paying down your student loans before they become due is also a great way to keep track of how much you are borrowing. I borrowed $2,500 a semester. It didn't sound like much at the time, but at graduation I had accumulated $20,000 dollars in loans. I honestly did not know what I owed in total until I received my first bill. That is the moment when the all of the magic money starts to feel like real money. It's not as fun when the bills coming to Mom and Dad's house are for you and not just them.

To avoid the sticker shock I experienced, keep track of how much you are borrowing. I'm putting particular emphasis on college loans at the moment because they aren't given to you as one lump sum like most other loans. When you buy a car using a loan, you finance the full $25,000 in one shot. When you finance your education, your debt builds up more slowly and can be more easily underestimated. As the old adage says, a frog dropped into a pot of boiling water will jump out, but one placed in water that is slowly brought to a boil will let itself cook. You're the frog, college loans are the slowing boiling pot of water.

Sallie Mae and the Department of Education make tracking your loans an easy task. They share the same website through Sallie Mae so all of your loan information can been seen at once. If you used a combination of government and private lenders, you will have to check each bank you borrowed money from, accessing your loan information through their website. This only takes a couple of extra minutes and after you look once and write down your number, you don't have to go back to update your information until you borrow money again. It requires very little effort to keep track of this very important number.

After graduation you are granted a six-month grace period before you have to begin making repayments on your student loans. The government feels this is ample time for you to find a job. Always the eternal optimist, this grace period never changes regardless of how many 18-26 year olds are waiting on the unemployment line. As a result, this six-month period becomes a game called Beat the Clock.

There are four ways the game ends. The happiest one involves you finding a good job within the six-month window allowing you to start your repayments on time and finding a comfortable place to live. The second and third solutions happen when you don't find a job. You either can be granted a hardship postponement on your loans until you find a job and move back in with Mom and Dad, or you can view this as an excellent time to go for your Masters degree. Just turn the magic money fountain back on and the repayments freeze while you flood yourself with more debt in school. This is only a practical option if you have done your research and know for sure that an advance degree is highly desirable in the field you are trying to break in to. It should also lead to higher pay. Otherwise, it is hard to justify the additional debt burden.

The last possible resolution to the game Beat the Clock is when you find a job that pays just enough to repay your loans, but not enough to do much else, and you end up back at Mom and Dad's place anyway. This is a very common outcome these days. According to the Pew Research Center, one-third of adults 18-25 live with their parents. It is especially common for students who spend a lot of money for an education in a field that doesn't pay a lot after graduation. Teachers are an excellent example. Teaching positions require a Bachelors degree at minimum, but to be competitive, a Masters is preferred. It is not hard for a teacher to take on $30,000 in debt only to make $42,000 a year. A situation such as this makes it hard to do things like rent an apartment, get married, or start a family.

The most important thing to remember about college loans is that you have to repay them. If you fail to make your payments on time, not only does the interest on the loans continue to accrue, but you are also racking up penalty fees. This can cause your debt obligation to balloon out of control. There is no way for you to escape the burden of repaying them. Burying your head in the sand and hoping they will be gone when you pull it out a few years later is a losing strategy.

As depressing as paying your loans may be, as victimized as you may feel by the "system," this is the situation you are in and the one you must face. The sooner you are able to accept the situation for what it is and begin making your payments, the sooner you will be free of them. Looking at your life 10 or 20 years down the road and realizing that you may still be paying for your education is depressing. Yet, letting your debt interest build and penalties mount on top of that can turn 10 years of repayment into 12 or 20 years into 25. Accept the hard truth for what it is and begin the agonizing process of pulling the Band-Aid off really slow. It's going to hurt.

Tip 3: Crushing College Loans

An investment in education pays dividends--
to the bank.

An article in the Wall Street Journal I read a while ago discussed how private lending companies are getting back into the student loan business. The default rate for student borrowers had dropped to a level acceptable for them and they were excited by the interest rates they could charge. The reporter interviewed one recent graduate who was excited because she was able to consolidate her $181,000 worth of student loans into one account. If you're thinking I must have put the comma in the wrong place or fat-fingered an extra zero, I did not. Though I wish I had.

Did her university hand her the deed to a condo in Miami along with her MBA? I hope so.

This recent grad was fortunate enough to land a good job after graduation. She stated that having consolidated her loan, she was on track to pay it off in 10 years. Using her ambitious goal, let's look at how screwed she is for the next decade of her life.

Consolidated Loan: $180,000
Interest Rate: 5% (she didn't say, so I'm giving her a generous assumption)
Loan Term: 10 Years

Total Interest Paid: $77,746
Total Cost of Education: $258,746

Roughly a quarter of a million dollars. That is what she spent on a Bachelors degree and a Masters of Business Administration (the most generic Masters you can get. Pick any college and look at their graduate programs, they'll have an MBA). According to a recent survey of CEOs, most MBA grads come out of college with the ability to make and read fancy spreadsheets but with little skill in the way of critical thinking that drives business innovation.

At least she didn't go for a Political Science degree. What can you do with that? (Yes, my B.A. is in Political Science. Live and learn.)

Few would argue that college is not worth the cost of admission. Studies show that a college graduate is likely to earn $500,000 more than their high school diploma'ed peers over the course of a lifetime. But our poor (no pun intended) MBA has already spent half of her lifetime bonus earnings potential before stepping foot into her professional career.

As a general rule, it is recommended that you only take on as much debt in college as you expect to make a year in your intended career. So, if your profession starts off at $45,000 a year, your total student debt should not exceed the $45,000 mark. Generally speaking, $180,000 is not what you will make a year with a Masters in Business Administration.

There are several places you can find average salaries for your chosen profession. One of these sites is glassdoor.com. Glassdoor even allows you to view the average salary of a particular job in your specific region, which is far more applicable than knowing the average salary nationwide. In addition to the web, many colleges and universities have begun offering this information through their business centers as a way of educating their students. Of course, both of these options require you to seek out this information. It is not simply handed to you when you declare a major.

Now back to our favorite MBA.

To make things easy, we'll call our MBA Jennifer. Jennifer will pay about $1,900 a month to stay on her 10 year plan. That is $1,900 she can't spend on a home, a new car, or any such luxury. For most people, this is an entire paycheck. Say Jennifer got an excellent job that pays $100,000 a year. Why not, she has her MBA after all. After the government takes their 25%, plus her healthcare, plus her social security, plus every other deduction that will be in there, Jennifer probably takes home about $65,000 each year. That's $5,400 a month, or $2,700 a paycheck.

After paying her college loans, Jennifer has $3,500 a month left. Sounds like a decent amount, except we haven't given Jennifer a place to live yet. If she would like a nice one bedroom apartment, in most metropolitan areas, that will run her anywhere between $1,500 and $3,000. We'll call it $2,200. Now Jennifer has a place to live and $1,300 left each month. Let me show you how quickly that $1,300 can disappear.

Car Payment:	$ 400
Car Insurance:	$ 105
Cell Phone:	$ 100
Cable/Internet:	$ 100
Credit Card:	$ 145
Electric:	$ 80
Coffee/Tea:	$ 70

Food:	$ 300
Total:	**$1,300**

These are only modest expense assumptions. Jennifer could easily find more things to spend her money on. What you see above is her financial reality for the next 10 years. 10 years is a long time. If she decides she hates the job she has, too bad. The only way she could hope to leave is to find another job that pays the exact same or more. $100,000 jobs for recent college graduates aren't exactly a dime a dozen.

Statistically, Jennifer is more likely to postpone major life events such as marriage, starting a family, or buying a home because of her debt burden. Studies have shown that individuals who take on a significant debt load in college tend to delay milestones in their lives because their monthly payments leave them with very little disposable income. Mom and Dad might tell the story of how they married at 21 and had you by 23, but they didn't have $181,000 in college debt.

Equally as troubling is how Jennifer decided to forgo the protections of federal loans and the protections they grant to their borrowers, for the convenience of having a single bill each month. Had she lost her job or suffered a pay cut while paying off federal loans, she would have several options available to modify her monthly obligations. Beyond simple deference and forbearance plans, the Federal Government offers numerous income based repayment plans that increase with the size of your paycheck.

Now, having her loan consolidated through a private lender, she would have no such recourse unless the company was feeling particularly generous that day. And we all know how often financial firms are generous.

Don't forgo the protections of federal student loans unless you absolutely have to. They generally have the lowest rates and offer you protections and repayment options that will not be available to you in the private market. Repayment plans can be tailored to a percentage of your income after graduation. If you find yourself without an income as you search for a job, repayments can be frozen entirely until you are able to resume paying. Good luck finding a deal like that in the private sector.

There was also another immensely important line missing in Jennifer's paycheck breakdown. Did you catch it? She's not saving a dime for retirement.

What Jennifer should do is reduce her contribution to her college debt and start contributing to a 401K. In order to take advantage of compound interest early in her career, Jennifer needs to get some money in the game. Waiting 10 years, until after she has eliminated all of her student loan debt, will put her far behind the curve. We'll touch on this more later.

So how does someone rack up so much student loan debt? I'm not sure what Jennifer's exact path to such an exorbitant debt was, but there are a few trends she might have followed.

Changing majors multiple times or late in your college career is the most assured way to increase your debt burden. Why is this? Because, you now have a new set of course requirements you must meet. That means what would have been a four year degree will now take you five or six years. Ouch.

Did you have a scholarship from your college or university? Maybe, you should read it again, carefully. Chances are it was valid for four years only. That fifth and sixth year will now be full price. Double ouch.

Want to keep your college loans as manageable as possible? Graduate in four years. Plain and simple. In order to make this a reality, work closely with your advisers when making your schedules. Don't just pick the classes that will let you sleep in until noon. Some classes are only offered one semester a year. Miss a key class the semester it's offered in your last year, and you'll be spending an extra year at your favorite institution of higher education (at full price).

Be careful if you fall out of love with your college of first choice and plan on transferring. You must make sure that your credits will transfer to your new college. If they don't, you will be forced to repeat classes you have already taken, and paid for. Already into your junior or senior year? You may want to tough it out where you're at. Pretty much no one will transfer more than 50% of credits required for graduation.

Lastly, don't drop classes after the last withdrawal day. Doing so will force you to cover the cost of that class, even though you will not be receiving credit for it.

True story - a student walked into his advisor's office to drop a class he was failing. The advisor informed him that he would be forfeiting several hundred dollars by dropping this class after the last allowable withdrawal date. The student, straight faced and completely confident, replied, "It's not my money. I have a loan."

This is the logic I'm fighting to eradicate. All loans are your money. The only difference is, it's money you have not made yet. But it's still your money. Do not let your college loans crush your future.

Work with your advisor to graduate in four years, limit making changes to your major, do not transfer colleges unless your credits transfer with you, and do not drop classes after their drop date. Do this and you will graduate in much better shape than our MBA Jennifer.

Tip 4: Don't Buy a Digital Farm

If you have ever bought a digital tractor for your digital farm or if you have ever bought digital gold coins with cold hard cash, **STOP**. This unbelievable practice is wasted money in its most pure form. It is hard to believe that a company that sells fake, online-only, not-worth-anything-in-real-life gold can be profitable. But for some reason it is insanely profitable. I have yet to speak with anyone who has 'fessed up to buying digital goods through a video game they're playing. However, the reality of the profits being collected by the makers of these games tells us that someone certainly is. Is it you? It's OK. This is a safe place, you can say it...

These "freemium" games, as they are known, are a plague on society. They are the ultimate form of Magic Money. They take your real money and give you imaginary products. What a business model. $10 for a JPEG image of a tractor? What a bargain. Especially considering you'll be able to harvest your virtual crops at a virtually faster rate. Does this sound ridiculous to anyone yet?

If you're struggling to pay for college, taking out loans, or just starting to make repayments on your loans, buying make-believe merchandise should be the last thing you do. If individuals who build enormous empires in digital worlds spent a third of that effort on building wealth in the real world, they could build a legacy to leave for their children.

These games distract us from building a real-world legacy by feeding on our need to compete against our peers. They have become a status symbol all their own. "What level are you on Candy Crush?" Such a question could make or break you at a social gathering. Something in the high double digits is considered acceptable. Anything below 30 makes it look like you're an outsider, not dedicated to the cause. Anything above 200 can bring gasps and skeptical looks. "Do you buy power-ups?" would most likely be the next question.

What a horrible position to be in. If you say no, you're a loser who can dedicate way too much time to playing a silly game involving crushing candy. If you say yes, then you are the sucker who pays real money for a virtual gain. Do yourself a favor. When it comes to virtual games, stop at mediocrity. This way you'll have enough social knowledge to still be fun at parties, but you won't be inclined to spend hundreds of real dollars to be in first place. In this case, bragging rights are expensive.

Often, when someone is having trouble paying off loans or starting a retirement account, a financial advisor will ask them if they drink coffee. When the individual says, yes they do, the advisor will then explain how a coffee a day can add up to hundreds of dollars a year (truth). This is commonly referred to as the "latte factor."

Please, never put yourself in a position where you meet with a financial planner and they are forced to explain to you the "digital tractor factor." I would hate to be on the receiving end of a lecture that is based on the principal that buying less **fake** stuff would allow you to buy more **real** stuff.

Your Receipt

1. Money from loans and money from a job are all the same.

2. Pay as much toward tuition as you can while still attending college to minimize debts.

3. Unsubsidized loans? Pay, at a minimum, the interest each month.

4. Keep track of your total loan

amount. Surprises are not good.

5.   Your total student debt should not exceed what you expect to make as a yearly salary in your chosen field of study.

6.   Buying digital goods can quickly derail even well intentioned financial plans and are completely illogical.

Chapter 2:

To Credit or Not to Credit

Tip 5: Magic Money

I started working when I was fifteen. I got a job at a roller skating rink handing out and fixing the skates. It paid minimum wage but gave me some spending money. Every two weeks I would roll into my boss's office and she would hand me my paycheck. In order to use any of this money, I had to take my paper check to the bank. Once there, I could either deposit the money or have it turned into cash. I usually split it down the middle, putting half in my savings account and taking half as cash.

I only worked around fourteen hours a week back then so my paycheck was never much more than $200. However, out of this $200 I was saving around $100 every two weeks. Not many adults save $200 a month and here I was at 15, doing just that. It was easy. I took the money I wanted to spend that week, put it in my pocket and the rest went into savings.

Every time I wanted to buy something, I had to look into my wallet and see if I had enough money. If I was out of cash, I had to pass on whatever I wanted to buy. That feeling - not having access to enough money to buy what you want at the exact moment you want it - has been completely lost on us. This generation has been blessed, and cursed, with Magic Money.

Magic Money is what I call debit and credit cards. No longer does anyone have to pass on buying what they want because they lack the cash. With my debit card I can instantly access all of the money in my checking account. Checking account running low? Not a problem. I have the ultimate Magic Money machine, my credit card.

The credit card is a viral pill lightly coated with the sweet sugar we call the "American Dream." This has made the destruction of our wealth easier to swallow. Every day our TV, our radio, our Facebook page, tells us we can have whatever our hearts desire. For the low, low payment of our financial security over the next several years, all of the pretty things can be ours. Simply sign on the dotted line to start living the dream. This message is further reinforced by our closest friends and family. After all, look at the pretty things they have. If they can afford it, we must be able to as well. Right?

Unfortunately, we have no way of knowing the financial situation of those around us. If we did, we would know that they most likely own very little and owe a great deal. They use their Magic Money to get everything they want.

Why do people spend their hard-earned money so freely? Because they have no physical relationship with it. The experience I had as a teenager, working at the skating rink and collecting a paper check, is gone. The culprit, another Magic Money element, is known as direct deposit.

Almost all employers use this method of payroll now. You supply them with a voided check and they use that to route your paycheck directly into your bank account. At no point do you get to see, feel, or smell the money you just spent countless hours working for. All you see is the number in your bank account grow (usually by less than we all hoped it would). You don't even have to wait in line at the bank on Friday afternoon to blow your paycheck at happy hour.

Looking at a number on a computer screen does not mean anything to us. Sometimes it's a big number, usually at the beginning of the month, and other times it's a small number, usually at the end of the month. The number Magically gets bigger and then, just as Magically, gets smaller. For most people the money in their bank account is used to pay for items they purchased months ago using their credit cards. I cannot speak for everyone, but for me, paying credit card bills is the least satisfying thing I can do during a given month. It's the same kind of feeling you have when you forget you owe someone money and then suddenly remember that you never paid them back.

Buying stuff is fun. You get to show it off to all of your friends. And, best of all, you can get it with Magic Money. There is no sense of loss on your part. In the past when you bought something, you handed the cashier physical dollars and in return they gave you the item you wished to purchase. An exchange was made. Even going back to the barter system of ancient times, an exchange was always made. One item was exchanged for an item of seemingly equal value. No caveman would have given you a mammoth fur for the promise of a saber tooth tiger in the future.

Today, you hand the cashier a plastic card, they swipe it through their machine, and you get your purchase as well as your card back. Wow. You got this amazing gizmo and they got nothing in return from you. You have surmounted the fundamentals of capitalism. Pure magic.

I could dig into the psychological aspects of getting something for nothing and how that influences the purchasing decisions of individuals today but it would not be half as effective as suggesting a simple exercise: carry cash for a week. Try starting with a modest amount. Anywhere between $50 and $100 is sufficient for this demonstration. See how long you can make this amount last.

Use this pocket money for non-essential items only. This is your coffee, gum, and lunch bought while at work money. Do not use this for fixed expenses. That would defeat the purpose of the exercise, which is to show you how quickly the non-essential items you purchase every day add up to real dollars.

The concept for this practical exercise comes from my own experience with Magic Money. I am a heavy coffee user. Rather than drink coffee to wake myself up, I drink coffee to function normally. While away from home I would buy my coffee wherever I was at that moment, be it Starbucks or Dunkin Donuts. My regular order of a Venti black, iced coffee cost me around $4.

To put my coffee habit into perspective, I will add some numbers:

One cup of coffee =	~$4
Cups purchased/week =	4
Cost per week =	$16
Cost per month=	$64

Yearly cost = $768.

Add one cup per week and the cost goes over $1,000 per year.

This expense never really sank in, though. I would hand the cashier my debit card and my Magic Money would cover my coffee addiction. I'm not even sure I looked at the price I paid on the register most days. My card was handed back to me, followed by my coffee. I gave the cashier nothing and I got a coffee.

One day, I happened to have some cash on me when I ordered my usual coffee. "4.25," the cashier said to me. I pulled out a five dollar bill and handed it to her. She put it in the drawer and handed me back a couple coins. I gave her a $5 bill and she gave me back pocket change. When I got my coffee, it didn't come with my $5 back. It was locked in her cash drawer forever. I had just made the decision that this coffee was worth sacrificing my $5 bill. A coffee.

I had made this transaction hundreds of times before, so why did this time feel so different? It was different because every other time I had used my Magic Money. I handed them my card, they would swipe it and hand it back to me. I had never given anything up for my coffee before. This time I felt the cost of my coffee. For once, I had to actually look at the price so I would know how much money to hand the cashier, dig in my wallet and retrieve my $5 bill.

Casinos have relied on the difference in feeling between actual money and play money to turn outrageous profits for years. If you've ever wondered why you cannot simply put cash on the table to play games, think about the scenario I just explained to you. If you put a $20 bill on the table and lost it, you would feel a lot worse than if you put a blue chip on the table and lost it. After all, you only lost one chip; you still have plenty of white and green chips. But in reality it was still $20.

Money is removed from the equation when you exchange cash for chips with the casino's cashier. A unique situation emerges. First, you gave a certain amount of money to the cashier and they gave you an amount <u>equal</u> to that value back in chips. Great. You didn't lose anything. Still feeling good.

Now, you begin to gamble with your chips and you start losing.

As you watch your pile of chips dwindle there may be a slight sense of disappointment, but do you really feel as though you're losing money? Not really. You can avoid feeling any sense of monetary loss at the gaming table by repeating one simple phrase to yourself, "Well, I already spent the money when I bought the chips."

Congratulations, you have avoided feeling as though you have lost any money, twice. You avoided it the first time by feeling as though you were only exchanging your money for something of equal value, and avoided feeling regret the second time by retroactively attributing your financial loss to the initial exchange of cash for chips. A convoluted train of thought, but one that our brains happily follow to avoid feeling guilt or loss.

That is why I recommend taking out cash at the beginning of the week and using only that cash to make purchases. Don't make any changes to your habits; just use your cash instead of your Magic Money. You will still be spending the same amount, but it will feel very different. Everything will **FEEL** expensive. You will have to <u>look</u> at the price, <u>look</u> at your cash, and make an **exchange**.

Imagine if you had to buy all of your coffee in one lump sum at the beginning of the year. How many people would be willing to pay $768 to drink as much coffee as they wanted for a year. Not many, myself included. Which is why I made the hard decision this year not to drink coffee outside of my home and office. Had I never made that purchase with physical dollars, I would have never taken the time to calculate exactly how much my cup of coffee was costing me. I would have continued using my Magic Money and would have continued to wonder where all of it magically went every month.

My in-laws have a fantastic way of managing the temptation of debt and credit cards. They give themselves an allowance. Each one gets $40 a week. Once it's spent, they don't resort to using their debit or credit card, they simply stop making purchases. If they spend less than $40, then it carries over into the next week. So if they only spend $20 one week, then the next week they will have $60 to spend. This money is not for groceries or other essentials, it's just fun money. This allowance is what they use to go out to dinner, buy something for themselves, spoil their grandkids, whatever they would like.

I recommend this method to anyone who has a problem controlling their spending. Which is, essentially, everyone. If you don't log onto your bank account regularly, it is easy to lose track of how much you are spending. This "allowance method" allows you to easily track your spending from month to month.

Escape the hold of Magic Money. See how long you can last on an allowance.

Tip 6: Get Smart

Get a credit card.

Surprised to get that advice following a chapter about the dangers of Magic Money? I know it can sound confusing but it is actually sound advice, and here's why. Credit Score companies like Equifax, Experian, and TransUnion, group borrowers into categories. For example, someone in their late teens and early twenties is categorized as a Student-Aged borrower. Your credit score then becomes a comparison of you as a student against your student-aged peers. They are not comparing you to the rest of the world. Your debt-to-income expectations cannot be accurately compared to someone in their sixties, so they don't try.

While part of this Student-Age Borrower group, you will get multiple offers to open a new credit account (a lot more than you would ever want or need). These are no frill cards that have relatively low borrowing limits. My first card had a $700 limit. I still have it because it would hurt my score to close it. These cards allow you to start building a credit history, which becomes much harder to do later in life.

If you do not take advantage of one of these offers in college, you will move into another category of borrower after graduation. You will not compare well to your peers in this new category if you have zero credit history. Most people establish some form of credit account before they're 25. These are the people you will be compared against.

Mom and Dad do not always know best in these situations. Some parents send their child to school with a credit card that the student is only an authorized user on. The credit card and credit history is entirely in the parent's name. Not only is this a liability to Mom and Dad (because you could easily run up their bill with books and booze), but it's actually a disservice to your future. While they feel they are protecting you from the predatory claws of the credit card companies, they are prohibiting you from building your own credit history that will stay with you through your life.

Look over the next few offers you get in the mail. You can discuss the offers with Mom and Dad if you value their advice, or use your best judgment. Try to find the one with the lowest interest rate and the highest borrowing limit. Low interest rates will help you if you ever have to carry a balance into the next month (though after reading this book I'm sure you never will). A high starting amount will keep the ratio of available credit and total debt at a level the credit companies consider acceptable. I'll give you a hint: it's nothing near 50%.

You also want a card with no annual fee. Why would you want to pay a company for the privilege to potentially earn interest off you? We know they won't earn any interest payments from you because you're building a debt-free mindset, but they don't. You may not be able to find a card that offers rewards, like cash back or airline miles early on. That's OK. Our goal is to build your credit so you don't need a co-signer just to rent an apartment.

If you're having a hard time finding a credit card company that will issue you credit, look to gas companies. They are often less stringent about issuing credit cards. Since gas for your car is something that should be included in your monthly budget, using your gas card to buy gas and making the payments in full each month should be a piece of cake.

Now opt-out.

Once you have chosen a credit card, opt out of receiving any more offers. You don't need them. Go to www.optoutprescreen.com to opt out of receiving more credit card offers. This won't stop companies from sending you offers if you sign up to receive information. So screw the free frisbee, or pen, or t-shirt, and don't sign up for anything because someone sitting behind a picnic table offered it to you in return for your contact information.

Need little and borrow less.

Once you have chosen your first credit card and decided which flashy design you're going to have on the front, the next step is to establish guidelines for yourself. The habits you establish now will be the ones you carry with you for the rest of your life. If you use your card to buy everything you want but don't have money for, you will instill a pattern of carrying a balance from month to month. This begins the downward spiral of having high monthly credit card payments, thus leaving you with less cash, forcing you to buy more on credit, further increasing your monthly payments and overall debt. Right on down the funnel-of-suck you will fall.

To avoid such a fate, limit your credit card purchases to items you need to buy anyway and already have the cash for. Recurring bills such as cell phones, electricity, cable and internet are a good place to start. These are relatively stable amounts that you are obligated to pay each month and should already be factored into your monthly budget. You should have no problem paying bills such as these in full at the end of the month when your credit card statement comes.

Regular charges and payments on your credit card are essential to establish a solid credit history. Opening a credit card, throwing it in a drawer and never using it will do nothing for you. It may be a smart move to leave your credit card at home if you're going to the mall and have no will power. But as a general rule, there needs to be activity on your credit account in order for the credit rating companies to establish a pattern of timely payments. Having a card and never using it doesn't make you a good borrower, only a good saver. You may think being a good saver would have a positive effect on your credit score, but as with a lot of things in life that make sense, it is not true.

My wife, in college, practiced the method I just described with her first credit card. She made small purchases that she already had the cash for and paid the full balance when her bill came at the end of the month. Her parents also listed her as the primary account holder on their cell phone bill, which is another trick that can be used to establish a credit history. As a result she had an excellent credit score and we took advantage of that when buying our first home. I, unfortunately, was not as wise with my spending. After getting my first credit card I was constantly looking at things I could buy with it. What did I find? I found a motorcycle. It could be mine for only $2,750. What a great deal. I had $250 I could spend in my checking account and a $500 credit card. All I needed was another $2,000. As fate would have it, on my desk sat a pre-approved credit card offer with a $2,000 limit. What a home run. I didn't think twice about maxing out both credit cards. Why would they offer me so much money if they thought I couldn't afford it?

It didn't take me long to realize that maybe my method of purchasing my motorcycle was not the smartest move. I made the minimum payments the first two months and noticed that my balance didn't seem to decrease at all. This was not going to work for me. I began making the largest payments I could to pay off the motorcycle as quickly as possible. It took me about six months. I basically worked that summer just to pay for my motorcycle.

The worst part of it all was that I left college having taken out about $20,000 in loans. $20,000 in loans broken down into eight semesters comes to - you guessed it - $2,500. I could have paid for that semester in cash had I not bought my motorcycle. Which means, if I could've done it that semester, I could've done it for all semesters. I could have graduated debt free.

Tip 7: Dude, Where's My Money?

One of the hardest aspects of managing money is keeping track of it. It's as though you awaken from an intense party binge at the end of the month - feeling a little guilty about what happened - and finding yourself flat broke. What happened while you were so busy tearing up the dance floor at your favorite club? How did you rack up so much debt that you can now only seem to make the minimum payment and still eat? Easily, that's how.

Imagine you're at a bar drinking with your friends, when you realize you didn't bring any money. Uh oh, you're "That guy." Your friends have already bought the first three rounds and now it is your turn to reciprocate. As you pat your pockets desperately searching for some misplaced money, a top-hat wearing man named Barry standing next to you at the bar offers to buy the next round for your friends - if you'll pay him back. You tell Barry that won't be a problem. You come to this bar with your friends every month. Barry smiles under his top hat and explains that next month you will have repay him the 4 beers he's buying you tonight and you will have to buy him a shot, as interest on the loan. Not a bad deal, you think. You get to save face in front of your friends for the added price of a shot next month.

A month goes by and you return to the bar with your friends. To be safe, you buy the first round this time. It also happens to be your friend's birthday, so you offer to buy the second round as well. As you hang out at the bar, Barry, with his top hat from last month, approaches you. He is here to collect on your deal.

After checking your wallet, you realize you spent the rest of your money when you bought the second round. You apologize to Barry and tell him you can't pay in full tonight, but you definitely will next month. Barry says this is not a problem. He goes on to explain, "Buy me a shot tonight, the interest you owe me, and we will be good for the month. Next month, you can pay in full by repaying me the four beers and a shot. If you do not have the money, you can always buy me another shot and extend the deal another month." You nod in agreement and buy Barry his shot.

Just like that, we so easily succumb to making minimum payments on our credit cards - month after month - because there is always another bar, another party, another hot new gadget that we must have. It is at that moment we rely on the generosity of the Magic Money man we all carry in our pockets, the top-hat wearing credit card company.

Minimum payments are a cancer that infects your overall financial health. It starts off small with no apparent side effects. Not until the tumor is so large that you feel yourself hemorrhaging money each month will you discover how unhealthy you've been living.

Tip 8: Small Number Shenanigans

Anyone who has purchased a car utilizing financing has most likely faced Small Number Shenanigans. Hey, for only $30 more a month you can get the fog lights and fancy rims you want. Instead of $300 a month, your payment would only be $330. You may look at those numbers and think, I can handle that. Oh, but now you are only $20 more a month from the deluxe package, which comes with leather heated seats and a sunroof. What a deal for only $50. The dealer then walks you over to the beautiful, polished, premium car in the showroom. This one is only $50 more a month, just $400. After sliding into the soft leather seats and retracting the sunroof, you are sold. Bring on the paperwork.

What gets lost in this interaction is the total cost of the upgrades you just purchased. (Don't worry, the finance manager will blow through these numbers like a freight train while trying to upsell you on even more expensive "care packages.") The first package, which had the low, low price of $30 a month, over the course of your five-year loan would cost you $1,800 more than you were planning on spending. The next upgrade, which came with additional improvements for only $20 (a total of $50 more per month) would cost you $3,000. The premium package you finally ended up selecting for $400 a month would cost you $6,000 more than the car you walked into the dealership intending to buy. If the dealer had sat across from you and said, "For $6,000 you could get the Premium Package," you more than likely would have said, "No." In fact, he probably did say just that, and then after you said no, pointed out how it would only be $100 a month. News flash. It's still $6,000.

The number only gets worse when you add sales tax and interest on the loan. With sales tax at 7% in New Jersey and auto loans hovering around 2%, the total outlay for these improvements would be about $3,275. You walked into the dealership intending to spend $18,000 but instead signed a contract that cost you $23,275. How did you let this happen?

Small Number Shenanigans is derived from the hidden power of financing. That power is the ability to make large purchases appear practical. Cars are not the only situation in which large purchases we might otherwise think twice about, are boiled down to smaller monthly sums. Furniture, home improvements, and even personal electronics are subject to Small Number Shenanigans.

We are bombarded by commercial after commercial that tells us, "You can afford this product. It's only a small monthly payment." Every time you hear this phrase your bullshit radar needs to flash bright red. Ask yourself if the reason they broke the total price into small pieces is because, if they told you the full price, you would tell them where to shove their product and change the channel.

If you are not willing to spend $240 on an aerobics video, you should not then be willing to make "six easy payments of only $39.99" for the same product.

The poor get poorer because businesses perpetually convince them that they can afford everything. A good mental trick to combat the effects of Small Number Shenanigans is to figure out the final cost of what you want to buy and then forget the monthly cost all together. If you are considering a furniture set that cost $5,000, ask yourself first if you are comfortable spending that much at that exact moment. Ask yourself if you have $5,000. If you don't have $5,000 right now, then the fact that you can finance this set for 24 months at $210 a month should have no bearing on your decision.

Another plague of having multiple purchases financed at the same time is that you never see all of your debt obligations together as a single number. You pay $380 to your auto lender, $210 to the furniture store, and $39.99 to the aerobics video company every month. You pay each one through that company's own website, never seeing more than what you owe to only that company. While $630 a month may be manageable for you, the damage is being done behind the scenes. You have amassed $28,815 in debt.

It happens that quickly. These are not outrageous financial assumptions. In fact, these may be modest assumptions for a large number of people who read this book. The only way to put financial burdens into perspective is to have them all written out in one place. A simple note pad or Word document will suffice. Next month, as you pay your bills, jot down your remaining obligations to each lender. If you were considering making another large purchase, this exercise may convince you otherwise.

When I decided to do just that, the number was upsetting. I had $25,000 in student loans, had just financed new windows for my house at $6,000, and bought a new car with $17,000 in financing. $450 went to the student loans, $300 to the windows, and $300 to the car. $1,050 a month was coming right out of my paycheck to satisfy items I had purchased months ago. I had no idea how brutal this number actually was because I was always looking at my finances from the wrong perspective.

I was looking at what I had left over from my paychecks at the end of the month. I saw that my wife and I had some extra money left over so we must be doing OK. I was oblivious to the fact that we were bleeding $1,050 a month. That's our entire mortgage payment. I could own a second home the exact same size as mine for the price I was paying in financing for other items. This is why it is essential that you list all of your debt obligations on a single sheet of paper. Doing so lays bare the truth behind Small Number Shenanigans, that several small numbers can quickly become one large number. Because it happens slowly, because it happens using Magic Money, you don't feel it until it becomes too much to handle.

So grab a pen and start writing:

LOANS	Loan Obligations	Percentage Rate	Monthly Payments
Student	$	%	$
Car	$	%	$
Credit Card	$	%	$
Other	$	%	$

Total Each Column:

What is your total debt? Is it a larger number than you realized? Now figure out what your seemingly manageable payments add up to for a month.

If these numbers are causing you stress, realize that you are on the path to repairing your financial situation. Understanding what kind of position you are in is only the first step. The hardest part is admitting you have a problem. Well, you have a debt problem. We all do. It is much harder to deny it when the numbers are staring you in the face.

The most important thing you have to do is stop making purchases on credit. You need to stop the bleeding.

Now that you have a clear understanding of what you owe and to whom, you have to make a plan for paying them all off. My favorite strategy comes from an old book called "The Richest Man in Babylon." In it, the author cites a debt reduction plan laid out for a debtor in Babylon. The plan was this:

Spend 70% of what you earn. You worked hard for your money and you should enjoy the fruits of your labor.

Save 10% of what you earn. You need to have a rainy day savings to avoid using debt the next time you fall on hard times.

Pay 20% of what you earn to your lenders. This will help you pay down your debts rapidly and continuously.

What debts you pay down first is up to you. There are different strategies recommended by different people. One method has you choose the debt with the highest interest rate. This makes the most sense because you are paying off the loan that you lose the most money to interest on.

However, if this is your largest debt, it can be discouraging if it takes you a long time to pay it off. It feels good to get a win. The plan I like best gives you the quickest win.

Pay off your debts in order from smallest to largest.

This method lifts your spirits by showing you that you can pay off your debts. After you pay off the smallest debt, the money that you used to send to that company gets rolled into the payments you send to the second smallest debt each month. This method is called snowballing payments.

Say you owe money to three different credit companies. To Company A, you owe 10,000, to Company B, you owe $5,000, and to Company C you owe $2,000. Each month you have a minimum payment of $100 to Company A, $50 to Company B, and $20 to Company C. If we set 20% of your monthly budget at $500, here is how you would pay off these debts.

Company A: $100 per month
Company B: $50 per month
Company C: $350 per month

As you can see above, you throw all of your extra money toward the smallest loan. At this rate, you would pay off your loan from Company C in six months. After that six months, the full $350 you are no longer sending to Company C gets snowballed into your payments to Company B.

Company A: $100 per month
Company B: $400 per month

Your monthly payment to Company B gets a huge boost. Using this method, Company B will be paid off in a year. And, after that is done, you guessed it, the full $500 goes toward Company A. This is the fastest way to becoming debt free.

Tip 9: Side Effects May Vary

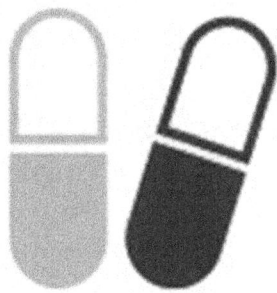

If you still watch TV, you may have seen a few credit card commercials. These commercials are pretty catchy and often show happy people getting generous rewards. They smile as they earn 3% cash back on their purchases and stroll along the beach on their perfect vacation. What is interesting about these commercials is how similar they are to pharmaceutical commercials.

Both industries show happy people about Mom and Dad's age using their products in ways that make their lives better. They can now do things they were previously unable to do. In the case of pharmaceutical companies, their customers can now run, jump, and play again like they did when they were 30. For credit card companies, their customers can now "afford" to take family vacations or buy fancy clothes and electronics. Below the rainbows and smiles lies the less glamorous truth.

After discussing all of the positive benefits of a drug, which is summed up in the first 5 seconds of a pharmaceutical commercial, the next 25 seconds is a list of the horrible potential side effects. These often include such gems as stroke, heart attack, and death. But while they're reading all of these worst case scenarios to you, they continue showing a happy couple kayaking down some rapids on the screen. Pharmaceutical companies frame all of the negative attributes of their drugs around positive images. This is done to minimize the impact of the horrible list of side effects they listed. Your brain compares the images and the words, concluding, "That sounds really bad, but look how happy those people are. I want to be that happy."

Suddenly, you forget the side effects they are required to list. What you do remember is what the drug does, because you really only paid attention for the first five seconds. You also remember that the people who you saw using the drug looked really happy. No sign of anal leakage to speak of between the two of them.

Credit card companies use this same type of framing. They show you their new 3% cash back promotion in the first five seconds. They know that's their hook. It sounds good to you so you keep watching. They then tell you that it also comes with six months zero percent APR (big surprise). They show happy people using their card out at fancy dinners and on beautiful vacations. They show Vikings conquering towns, and saving the people with their credit cards. They show you that happiness can be bought, and it can be bought with their credit card. "So You Can," is one company's tagline. Even though you really can't which is why you need a credit card to be able to "can."

Unlike pharmaceutical companies, credit card companies don't have to list any potential side effects. This is in spite of the fact that the side effects of excessive debt are well known. If they did provide a list, their commercials might sound a lot different.

Side effects of excessive debt use may include: insomnia, irritability, depression, feelings of despair, homelessness, divorce, high blood pressure, weight gain, indigestion, weight loss, and decreased sexual desire. As always, ask your financial planner if the benefits outweigh these risks.

Anyone else think they'd sign up a lot fewer card users?

Commercials are designed to show you happiness as a direct result of purchasing a specific product. Coke, with "Open happiness" and McDonalds with "Happy Meals," make this correlation rather blunt. But we cannot blame companies for advertising. Advertising is how we learn most products exist at all. What we have to blame is our culture's insistence that we must own <u>one of everything</u>.

If you give someone an iPhone, they're going to want Beats headphones. It's just the way we are wired. We have always wanted for more. The only difference is credit cards have given us the ability to have more while still earning the same income. It is up to you, the consumer, to only purchase what you can afford <u>today</u> and not what you <u>hope</u> to have money for in the future. Happy credit card debtors are a myth. A myth perpetuated by our reluctance to talk about debt.

We have to work with credit card companies. Our society has evolved around credit ratings and credit scores. Is it fair? Does it make sense? No and no. Unfortunately we don't always make the rules for the world we live in. The best thing to do is play by the rules. You know how to beat them at their own game: only charge recurring expenses that are already included in your monthly budget. Do not charge impulse purchases. Pay your bill, in full, every month.

Tip 10: Trust Us, We're the Credit Card Company

Spend today
Money from tomorrow
And pray tomorrow
Pays like today

One of the more surprising aspects of the credit issues we inherited from Mom and Dad is the overwhelming faith people have in these companies. The same people who don't trust the Congressmen they elected a week ago throw their full faith behind a credit card company that sent them an unsolicited offer in the mail.

Zero percent interest for six months? Sure. After all, you can pay off the balance before the six months is up and you will have simply borrowed that company's money for free. It seems like a great plan and I'm sure we both have said something similar to ourselves at one time or another. What often happens, however, is we run up a balance we find difficult to pay back within that zero percent interest window. After the six month grace period, zero percent instantly becomes 20-25%. Even worse, some companies charge you back interest on the entire loan amount for failing to pay in full before the end of the grace period. What does that look like, you ask?

You buy a sofa for $2,000. The business is offering 0% financing and zero payments required for one year. After that year, the interest jumps to 15%. In your mind, this means that they will **start** charging interest after a year. This is false. If you do not pay off the couch in that first year, which they don't require you to do, then the full interest, which has been compounding monthly since you "bought" the couch, reattaches to your balance. You now will owe $2,321.51 cents for your $2,000 couch. Worse yet, the interest continues to run up the cost of your couch while you spend the next 2 years actually paying off the couch.

This is the position most people find themselves in.

How can I say with such certainty that we often betray their promise to themselves? Credit card companies make money hand over fist. They don't accomplish this by giving away interest free loans to everyone for six months. They do it by getting everyone to sign up for their cards with sexy, low introductory rates that seduce you into thinking they are a good idea. It's time to call the Sirens for what they are, temptresses trying solely to bring your financial ship crashing upon their shores. Your wealth spread across their beach, you're left with only a broken ship to sail into retirement. Most will sink.

This is not to say that credit cards are all bad. They are a strong way to establish a positive credit history. Doing so enables you to borrow money at the lowest available rates. When borrowing large sums of money, as most will do when they buy a house using a mortgage, having a good credit score can save you tens of thousands of dollars over the life of the loan. Also, today's employers regularly check a candidate's credit score as part of the application process. You can't even get an interview in some cases if you have a poor credit rating. This is especially true if you plan on entering an industry requiring some form of fiduciary responsibility. If you spend your whole life shunning credit cards, you will be hard pressed to establish any form of credit history.

There is one caveat to this advice. The decision to open a credit account should be on your terms, after careful consideration. Not simply because you were "Pre-Approved."

Establishing good credit using credit cards requires following one rule: charging only what you know you can afford, regardless of what the total available credit limit is. A card with a $10,000 line of credit does not mean you can safely charge $10,000 on it. This is the credit world equivalent of giving you enough rope to hang yourself with. They're kind enough to tie the noose before handing you the rope, too.

Before you charge any amount, consider how long it would take you to save $10,000 because it will take you at least twice as long to pay off that amount. Paying down debt is not nearly as fun as saving money, so we tend to be less eager to do so. And face it, we Americans already don't save anything.

One of the more predatory strategies lending companies utilize is the employment of data aggregation companies to identify different categories of borrowers. These categories help them identify who is most in need of what type of financing. If you use payday lenders, if you're late on multiple accounts, if you have unpaid medical bills, this data is sold to credit card companies so they may target advertisements toward you. This allows them to charge higher rates to people who are known to be heavy users of credit. Their aim is not to help you get out of debt (though that's what the ad probably says). They just want to be the ones earning the high interest rate instead of your current lender as you spiral toward bankruptcy.

How can anyone resist these offers? Just when you are faced with the reality that you have taken on too much debt, along comes a new offer in the mail. They might as well write, "We see you suck at managing credit, so we're offering you more credit at a higher interest rate," on the envelope. Who knows, they might even see a spike in business if they did that.

Studies show we are more willing to talk about politics and our weight than we are credit card debt. So a new offer of credit from a company that will help us bury our heads in the sand a little longer is impossible to refuse. Think about it. When was the last time you heard someone talk about losing weight or how lousy Congress is? Now think, when was the last time you heard someone talk about how their crushing debt is their fault? Probably never.

This is because our society puts so much pressure on people to have nice things and show them off. If people knew how much debt you were in, the illusion of success would evaporate. It is sad how people would rather suffer through financial ruin secretly than moderate their spending publicly. As though losing your house to foreclosure and having your car repossessed screams success.

A bankruptcy lawyer once gave a presentation to a large convention of bankers. Her lecture, supported by vast amounts of research data, surmised that if banks cut off the riskiest 10% of borrowers they lend to, they could avoid 80% of their bad loans. This suggestion caused quite a stir in the group until one banker finally interrupted the commotion by stating that the most vulnerable 10% represents the bank's highest profit margin. His explanation for this phenomena - those borrowers have an "appetite" for debt. Do you have an appetite for debt?

Those with an appetite for debt can be described as individuals who are consistently making minimum payments while continuing to take on additional debt burdens. The goal is to drive your monthly debt up to the point where your entire disposable income is used to pay debt. They're financial vampires who have you chained in their dungeon. They bleed you as much as they can to feed their lust without killing you, so they will have you to bleed again next month. If they do bleed you to financial ruin, it costs them a little extra to dispose of your body and replace it with a new one. But sometimes this happens. Vampires aren't perfect. It's just the cost of being a bloodsucker.

The only way to escape the dungeon is to save some of your financial strength each month until you have enough of it to break the chains that bind you. The banks do not care about you. There are no hero vampires in this story that care more about the human race, Volvo's, and glitter body paint, than financial gain. They will all chain you in their financial dungeon and bleed you as long as you show them you are vulnerable. The only way to overcome this is to slay your first vampire; pay off one of your debts.

Paying off your first credit card can give you the confidence you need to take on the rest. The incredible release you will feel as the weight of debt is lifted from your shoulders will be the motivation driving you to continue paying off your debts. It will give you the strength to forgo purchasing those things you want to buy now for the reward of financial security in the future. This is why I recommend starting with your smallest debt first when you make the decision to start living debt free. It gives you a quick victory you can use to fuel the rest of your Herculean effort.

Tip 11: Refinance at Your Own Risk

If you have multiple loans with various interest rates, refinancing is always a good idea, right? Wrong.

Refinancing is a term you have probably heard quite a bit. I even talked about it early in this book. Remember our favorite MBA Jennifer? She refinanced her $181,000 in student loans, some federal and some issued by private banks. I'm sure she either saw an advertisement or was told by an associate that refinancing could lower her interest rate and make her payments easier by only having to pay one bank.

Was this the right move for her to make? Yes and no. As we talked about earlier, by refinancing her college loans with a private bank Jennifer forfeited the protections her government issued debt provided. A better option for her would have been to consolidate her private loans into one account but leave her government loans with the government. This would leave her with two payments to make each month but she would have the protections of federal loans for at least half of her money.

If all of your student loans are with the federal government, leave them alone. Even if your interest rates are slightly higher than what you could find through consolidating them, the protections they offer you outweigh the reward of a lower rate. I hope that you graduate and find a job that pays sufficiently enough that you never need to use the government graduated repayment plans. But that is not the reality we live in today. Keep your protections.

You're probably wondering if you should consolidate other debts you may have. Didn't Mom and Dad take out a home equity loan to pay off other debts they had? They most likely did. That does not mean it was a smart move.

Home equity loans are considered *secured credit*. Secured credit is a loan supported by something you own. These are mortgages (backed by the house), auto loans (backed by the car), and the like. Here's an easy way to think about a secured loan: if there is something the bank can take away from you for not paying, it's a secured loan.

The other end of the debt spectrum lays *unsecured credit*. Unsecured credit typically comes in the form of credit cards and, you guessed it, college loans. With unsecured debt, there is nothing that can be taken away from you (at least not without a court order). You never want to pay off unsecured debt with secured debt.

When you pay off unsecured debts with secured debts you are putting things you own at risk of being taken away. If you use a home equity loan to pay off credit card debt, you now risk losing your home. Before, with unsecured debt, you only risked the credit card company smearing your credit score. The same goes for college loans.

College loans are unsecured debt. No one is going to roll up to your apartment in the middle of the night and take your car away because you failed to pay your loan the past few months. However, if you take out a title loan (a loan backed by the value of your car) to pay off your college debts and you fail to make payments on that debt, you can expect to have your car repossessed.

Unsecured debt typically carries a higher interest rate than secured debt. There is a reason for this. With unsecured debt, the bank is holding most of the risk. They're extending you credit based entirely on your reputation (credit score). They can offer lower rates on secured credit because their financial risk is mitigated by whatever asset you used to guarantee payment. When deciding whether or not to refinance your debts, consider who presently holds the most risk, you or the bank, and how that would change if you refinanced.

Your Receipt

1.   Magic Money makes your finances less tangible.

2.   Purchasing an item on credit is not the same as *buying* that item.

3.   Giving yourself an allowance can make your money feel more real.

4.   Your credit score can have long-term effects on getting certain jobs and owning a home.

5.   Build your credit by only using your credit card for fixed monthly expenses. Pay them off monthly.

6.   Do not carry balances or make minimum payments.

7. Small monthly payments are used to make large, unattractive purchases seem reasonable. Focus on the total cost, including interest.

8. Spend 70%, pay 20% toward debts, save 10%.

9. Excessive debt has very real side effects.

10. Credit companies are not your friend, do not have your best interest at heart, and will happily bankrupt you while making a profit.

11. Secured debt, they can take whatever you used as collateral (house, car, motorcycle, diamond ring, etc.

    Unsecured debt, your assets are protected from everything (except a court order)

Chapter 3:
Bigger Purchases, Bigger Holes

Tip 12: Find Your Joneses, Let Them Win

Covet thy neighbors' possessions,
Inherit thy neighbors' debt.

We always hear about "Keeping up with the Joneses," but no one seems to describe themselves as a participant in the race to keep up. News Flash: if you have credit card debt month after month and can't get out of it, you've already entered the race. To stop chasing the Joneses and get out of your debt situation, you first have to figure out who exactly you're chasing.

We all have Joneses in our lives. Most often, they go by different names. For you, the Joneses could be Mom and Dad. For someone else, they could be a neighbor, coworker, or celebrity. To figure out who your Joneses are, think about who in your life always has the latest and greatest. The person who, no matter how big your TV is, theirs is always bigger. If, after seeing this person or people, you're left feeling their life is better than yours because they have a particular item you don't, you have found your Joneses.

Whoever your Joneses are, imagine all of their beautiful possessions as a mirage in the desert. You can see it on the horizon and decide to use all of your strength to get there. As you crawl the final hundred yards approaching your destination, to your dismay, you find out none of it was real. All of the beauty has evaporated. The happiness you thought you'd find at the end of the desert sand was a figment of your imagination. And you, having used all of your strength to make it to this promised land, will perish with the illusion.

Think about all of the nice things those around you own that you would love to have. Perhaps one of your friends owns a nicer car than you, or even better, a nice boat. How great life would be if you could have those things too. Heck, with a decent credit score you could drive a nice car and cruise around in a boat of your own on the weekends. But at what cost to your future?

We need to reset our perspective when we look at the nice things of those around us. We often look at people with a lot of fancy toys and think, "Wow, they've made it." When what we should really think is, "Have they made it up?"

How much of what you see do they actually own? Probably not much, if anything at all.

Rather than possessing the title to any of their property, they possess thousands of dollars in loan obligations. If that doesn't sound as sexy as the new luxury car looks, that's because it's not. We need to look at the spending of our neighbors and think, "I hope that's not all financed. I would hate to have that burden." Reframing our perceptions is not easy. Every day I see the same ads on TV you do and have the same feelings of desire. I do not pretend to be above the fray in any way. What I do remind myself is that I haven't EARNED it yet.

Every day, companies try to convince us that we do not need to wait to buy their product. No need to have all the money now, just give them a small down payment and they will help you finance the rest. This is an excellent deal for them and a lousy one for you. Not only do they get to sell you their product at what they feel is a fair market price but they also get to earn interest on your purchase for the next 6, 12, 18, or 24 months.

Let me throw an example your way. You are desperate to get the latest HD TV. Unfortunately, it costs $2,000. That night as you watch your old, standard, HD TV, a commercial advertising this new product offers you a 12 month financing deal. Awesome. No money down and only $185 a month. You can afford that right now. Let's see how you make out in the end.

Initial Price: $2,000
12 Monthly Payments of: $ 185
Total Cost: $2,220
Effective Interest Rate: 11%

That HD TV just cost you $220 more than it cost the person who walked in and paid cash for it.

Why do the rich get richer while the poor don't? Because the poor pay more for goods than the rich do. Imagine if you walked into the same store and a sign on the wall said, "Poor and middle-class: Please add 11% to all prices advertised." You would turn around and walk out. Yet we make purchases this way every day.

"Would you like to sign up for our store credit card and save 20% on your purchase today?" "Absolutely not," should be your only answer to that question. Let's lay the reason why on the table.

New Washer-Dryer Set:

Initial Item Cost:	$3,000
Store Credit Card Savings:	20%
Total Cost Put on Store Credit Card:	$2,400

What a great deal. You saved $600. It is hard to believe the store can stay in business offering such great deals. The truth is they would not be able to if they were giving away discounts so freely. So how do they do it?

You have now put $2,400 on a credit card that has an interest rate somewhere around 15-18%. We will call it 15%. Making minimum payments of $48 on the card, it would take you 16 years and cost you $2,913 in interest alone. Not only would this wipe out your entire 20% savings but it cost you double the amount of the initial purchase.

Total Effective Price with Interest: $5,313.

You're probably yelling into the book, "I would pay off the balance the first month I got the bill. The store wouldn't earn any interest off of me and I would still save the 20%." To which I say, if you have the cash on hand, just pay cash. It is not worth opening another credit card every time someone offers you a discount. Also, as much as you mean it in the moment, that you will pay that bill in full as soon as you get it, the minimum payment can look much more attractive after you've already spent some of that $2,400 you set aside a month ago.

The Joneses in your life don't pay the full amount due when they get the bill. That is their secret. If they did, they wouldn't be able to buy the next totally awesome, must-show-off thing that comes to market. When they finally do pay off a purchase, they immediately look for the next thing to spend their $300 a month on. Paid off the boat? Great, now I can buy a motorcycle. Paid off the car? Fantastic, let's buy a new one. And on and on it goes; the 21st century circle of life. Maybe I can ask Elton John to write a remix and give it away with the digital copy of this book.

If you're still having trouble accepting the idea that the Joneses are truly broke and chasing them will only lead you into the same situation, ask yourself this question: If you lost your job, what would you get to keep and what could the banks take away? If you would get to keep nothing and the banks would be able to take everything, you are racing the Joneses.

Tip 13: "Affordable" Leases

We hear it all the time, "New *affordable* prices." But what do they mean? Affordable how? Affordable to whom? It would be unrealistic to think that everyone watching the Mercedes-Benz commercial can actually afford the new "affordable" leases. So then why call it affordable?

The answer lies in our society's new definition of affordable. It used to mean you could buy and own an item, but now it's defined as, "one's ability to make the payment this month." It says nothing about owning the item, nothing about your ability to pay for it the month after next, simply that you can pay what the seller is asking at this precise moment. We should not be comfortable with this new definition. This redefined "affordable" belies its intended meaning. If something is affordable, it should remain affordable to you indefinitely.

Getting laid off next week? It should still be affordable.

Affordable is not a generic term that can be applied to any item uniformly. When companies try to slap the affordable label on every product they offer they are treating it in just that way. What is affordable for you may not be for me and vice versa. The most egregious perpetuators of the false definition of affordable are car companies offering their leases.

Leases somehow pose a magical ability to make cars that are generally unaffordable, affordable. Wow. What magic. How can something that wasn't affordable to me before suddenly become so? The short answer is it can't. The only thing that changes is how they manipulate the definition. This new definition is so powerful it can take something already unaffordable, make it more expensive, and call it affordable. They make you feel like they're giving the car away. Let me assure you, they're not. They're making much more money off of you in the long run.

While your monthly payments are lower than if you had financed the car, one of two things happens when your lease runs out. Either you love the car and end up buying it anyway or you decided to get a new lease. Those are your only options. I suppose you could forgo a car altogether and walk everywhere, in which case my eco-friend you can skip the rest of this chapter.

If you do fall in love and choose to buy your car at the end of the lease, then you will have to pay well above the original price of the car when all is said and done. Say you leased a 2012 Jeep Grand Cherokee for $415 a month. The SUV's original sticker value was $38,000. Over the course of your 36 month lease, you will have paid $14,940 toward the Jeep. If you decide to buy the SUV at the end of the lease however, the dealership is not going to charge you the sticker value minus what you've already paid, which would be $23,060. No, no, no. They are going to charge you the current market value of the car. In this case, a 2012 Jeep Grand Cherokee with 30,000 miles can cost $30,000. If you buy this Jeep after the lease expires, you will have given the dealership $7,000 dollars to make the car "affordable" for you. That is seriously broken logic.

Say you decide not to purchase your lease at the end of the term, but instead, get a new lease. How would your finances compare to someone who bought a car of equal value after 10 years? Say I buy a Honda Accord with financing for five years at a cost of $400 a month. You lease the same model car every three years at $300 a month. At the end of 10 years, my car will have cost me $24,400. Your three cars, over the same time, will have cost $36,000. When we both go to get our next car, I would be able to sell mine for at least $5,000 and you wouldn't have anything to sell. If you add the $11,600 difference in total payments over 10 years to the $5,000 my car is still worth, the total amount you would have spent is $16,600 more than I did. How "affordable" do those leases sound now? Not very.

It is time to go back to the true definition of afford: to have enough money to pay for. If you can't afford to buy it, you certainly can't afford to lease it.

Tip 14: More House, More Stuff

Too much emphasis is put on the size of and amenities in our homes, not enough on the love and comfort provided within its walls.

If you have never traveled abroad and seen how people in other countries live, though I hate to give validity to reality TV, there are several shows that can give you a glimpse into how others in the world live. The best shows star Americans looking for a home in another country. What the American house hunters quickly have to come to grips with is the size of the homes. The bedrooms are smaller, bathrooms are smaller, not all of the closets are walk-ins, and kitchens have room for cooking but little else.

American consumers buy substantially more items per person than any other country. As a result, we need extra room to put all of our stuff. As we get more stuff, our houses get bigger to store it all. Too much space - buy more stuff. Too much stuff - buy more space. And so the cycle continues until you go broke or die. At which point your children try to pick up where you left off.

When my wife and I first moved into our home we blew through money at a rate faster than I could have ever imagined. We suddenly had a lot of open space in our new home. So we filled it. Looking back on how quickly the money flew out of our hands, the realization came to me that my wife and I were trying to have everything our parents have. Our parents were our Joneses. We were trying to accumulate in three months what our parents had purchased over their lifetimes. It was a game we were bound to lose. Fortunately, we realized what we were doing before we buried ourselves in debt and decided to spread our purchases out over a longer period of time. (We also began to run out of space.)

I don't feel this is a flaw unique to us. By the time we are old enough to understand what possessions are, our parents generally have a lot of them. So we grow up thinking, "I'm supposed to have all of this stuff." But when saddled with college loans and an unenthusiastic job market, it can be hard to obtain the same level of comfort our parents have achieved.

It is important to remember that moms and dads started off small. My parents started in a mobile home. They didn't rush out to take on a huge mortgage and start financing furniture to fill it up with as soon as they moved out on their own. But now, if we are unable to do just that, we feel as though we have been left behind and are taught that it is acceptable to use credit to try to catch up.

This is where the finance companies move in to help fill that void between our income and our expectations. Credit companies help people with too much stuff buy more space and those with too much free space buy more stuff. Unfortunately, we are doing so by spending the money we <u>hope</u> to make tomorrow, today.

MTV Cribs was one of the best demonstrations of the infinite need for excessive space. It showed the ridiculousness of buying huge houses. The houses were somewhere around 15,000 square feet, had 30 rooms, Olympic size swimming pools, and all of this for 3 occupants, usually the owner, his girlfriend, and their tiny dog. Countless times you would hear them say, "We don't really use this room too much." Which is understandable. With that many rooms you almost have to schedule visits to each one to make sure you use them all at least once a month. Two people don't need five bathrooms and six bedrooms. Society has spent the past several years trying to convince us that, not only do we need it, but we can have it - with debt.

It's not that your family <u>needs</u> six bedrooms, it's that you <u>can have</u> six bedrooms. Somehow we've come to equate "can" with "should." This mindset is represented in the 90% of lottery winners who ultimately declare bankruptcy. They suddenly find themselves in a position where they "can" have anything they want. So society tells them they "should" have it. No one wants to look cheap in front of their friends. And doesn't mom or dad deserve a new car?

Being practical is not being cheap. If you only have three family members in a home, you probably do not need more than three bedrooms. Larger homes are not just more expensive when you buy them, they are more expensive for life. They cost more to heat, cool, maintain, and repair. So, before you stretch your budget to the max to buy a huge home, seriously consider if it is the home you need, or the home you want to need.

Tip 15: If I Had a Million Dollars...

So many of us like to throw this idea out when discussing finances at social gatherings. "If I had a million dollars I would . . ." The dreamers say things like buy a bigger house, a faster car, a boat, an airplane, etc. Basically toys, large and expensive, but toys nonetheless. In this sense, they want to use money to buy happiness. They see owning these new toys as a key to happiness. The problem with this line of thinking is that there will always be a faster car, a bigger house, or a fancier boat than the one you would buy. If your sense of accomplishment was based around your spacious million dollar home, it would evaporate when you went to your first dinner party at your neighbor's three million dollar estate.

This never ending cycle of needing bigger, faster, more expensive things was clearly demonstrated in a jailhouse interview with Lee Farkas. For those who do not recognize the name, probably most of you, Farkas was one of the only bankers successfully prosecuted in 2008 following the economic downturn. Despite having a sea plane, a garage full of cars, multiple homes, and a jet, he refers to himself in the interview as a pauper among his group of friends. Most of us, if we owned a jet, several exotic cars, and a few homes would not define ourselves as being poor. So how is it that Mr. Farkas could look at himself that way?

As you begin to step into higher wealth brackets, you begin to hang out with wealthier people. If you buy a million dollar home, it's going to be in a million dollar neighborhood. You will go to the same gym and shop at the same mall as those people in your community. If you squeezed into this wealth bracket by the skin of your teeth, you will then start to compare yourself to those around you. A feeling of poverty will start to control you as you struggle to match your lifestyle to theirs.

Of course, not all individuals feel they need everything bigger, faster, stronger. Some have more noble uses in mind for a million dollar windfall. These are things such as paying off their mortgage and other large debts, or saving it for their children's college fund. Obviously, when compared with buying new toys, these are more financially responsible choices. Realizing that your debts are something to be rid of as fast as possible is a great step.

The problem is, regardless of how noble your plans are, the odds of you conveniently coming into a million dollars are pathetically small. The lottery is just a tax that people don't recognize as a tax. You voluntarily give the government $2 a week, $104 a year, for the 0.000025% chance you could win millions. The government keeps half of what they take in and gives the other half to the winner (and then they tax that half). So when you see the lottery jackpot reach $450,000,000, know that the citizens of that state just gave an equivalent amount to the government voluntarily.

But good news. You don't have play the lottery and win to fall into a pile of money. You can pay down your debts, pay for a wedding, save for your children's education, and own your house sooner than you think. All you need is a clear plan and enough mental fortitude to follow through with it. It starts with realizing how your money moves through your pockets.

Tip 16: Find the Holes

For most people with crushing debt, their finances flow this way:

1)   Paycheck
2)   New Toys
3)   Debts
4)   Savings/Investments

When your money follows this path it causes a couple of problems. The first problem is that people look at their whole paycheck think that the amount they see is what they have to spend. That is FALSE. The money from your paycheck is not just for today, tomorrow, or the rest of the month. It is for this month and every month after until the day you decide to retire.

If you buy toys and run up debts with your money before putting any of it into savings, then you are borrowing against the security of your future to finance today. It is the recipe the majority in this country use to cook their lives into what they think will be something palatable. It is the recipe for financial ruin.

There is a better way, an easier way. Take your paycheck and lop off 30%. The remaining 70% is what you can spend. Let's say you make $2,000 a paycheck. You would be allowed to spend $1,400 of it. The remaining 30% gets broken up between paying off your debts while at the same time setting money aside for savings. 20% would be put toward paying off your debts, while 10% would go right into savings.

You may wonder why you shouldn't put the entire 30% toward paying off your debts. The 10% you put into savings is your safety net. Without any money in the bank, you risk going right back into debt after encountering an unexpected large cost. Most people suggest a cushion of at least three months worth of expenses. Using the same paycheck and expenses as above, $2,800 a month in expenses would require $8,400 in savings. While this may sound substantial, if you save 10% of your pay every month it would take you less than two years to build up your cushion. If you want to add a little extra security to your life, save enough to cover six months worth of living expenses.

The easiest way to do this is to have 10% of your paycheck direct deposited into a bank account separate from your primary one. Keep the checkbook associated with it someplace safe, label it "For Emergency Use Only," and do not get a debit card for it. A debit card would make it too easy to access your rainy day fund.

After you reach your three month threshold, this same 10% should be directed into a dedicated retirement savings account. Either subscribe to your employer's 401k plan (especially if they offer a match on your contributions), or start your own Individual Retirement Account (IRA). I'll cover more on retirement accounts after we finish discussing how to crush your debt.

Getting back to the ambitions you had for your one million dollars, I hope you are starting to realize it is better to plan to be rich than to plan to be poor and hope for riches. The hardest part is learning to turn off the noise around you. Every day on TV and radio we are bombarded with ads that tell us we can buy whatever we want. Even if you have bad credit or no credit, not a problem, they can help make it WORSE. Magic Money is all around us. Just wave the magic pen across the line at the bottom of the page and POOF, that new car, house, TV, or college degree is yours.

What we don't see in ads every day are the college graduates who are struggling with their bills. The moms and dads who every month rack their brains to figure out how they are going to pay their debts and still feed themselves. They want so desperately to fill their buckets with wealth and security but every time they give in to the desires that marketing builds in us, they poke another hole in their bucket. This is why people who struggle to control their small purchases think saving money is impossible.

If you're trying to fill a bucket that looks like Swiss cheese with water, it will always drain faster than you can fill it. Likewise, if you try to build wealth while poking holes in your savings with credit card debt, you will find it increasingly frustrating and conclude that the effort must be hopeless. I'm here to tell you it is not hopeless. You just have to figure what you are doing that is putting so many holes in your bucket.

Unbelievable as it may seem, there is an amazing tool that has been developed that can help you combat the perils of Magic Money, and it's FREE.

Mint, an online financial tracking tool developed by Intuit, syncs up to your various bank accounts and compiles all of your data into one place. Want to know how much you spend on coffee a month? Simply sync your accounts to Mint and it will download all of your transactions. Type the word "Coffee" into the search bar. Mint will then show you all of the coffee shops you buy from and how much you spend on average at all of them each month. You can then go on to set a budget for coffee, which will enable Mint to email you when you have reached the limit you set.

Want to keep track of how much you owe and to whom? Enter the loan information into Mint and it will track your payments and total debts. It can even help you stay on track with repayment plans by alerting you if you fall behind on your set goals.

I do not have any type of affiliation with Intuit or their program Mint, aside from being a frequent and passionate user. I say this so you don't become discouraged from using it. I recommend this program wholeheartedly as the easiest, most effective way to demystify your financial life. Magic Money simply becomes money once again. You can see how it enters your life and through what gaping holes in your pockets it escapes.

The Mint program makes its money through the recommendation of various banking and investment companies. They look at what you currently have and present you with offers that might help save you money or provide you with a better retirement savings. But keep in mind that these are all advertisements. Mint, while an amazing financial tool, is not in your fiduciary corner. There is no one on the other side of the screen making sure these offers will actually save or make you more money. If you are presented with something that looks like a good deal, do your own due diligence. Don't just do something because Mint told you to.

Your Receipt

1. Figure out who your "Joneses" are. Let them "win."

2. Financing purchases results in paying more for an item than someone who paid cash.

3. Your "Joneses" don't pay cash for anything.

4. Clearly define your *Wants* versus your *Needs*.

5. Bigger homes mean bigger expenses, and not just in terms of mortgage payments.

6. How wealthy you feel is directly related to who you compare yourself to.

7. Several small purchases can erode savings just as quickly as one large purchase.

Chapter 4:

Retirement Not Just Mom and Dad's Problem

Tip 17: The "R" Word

Who wants to think about retirement? Even though commercials every day on TV talk about saving for retirement, we still think those commercials are for Mom and Dad, not us. They ask pressing questions like, "How much will you need in retirement?" The most popular responses from Generation X are, "How should I know?" and "Who gives a shit?"

I'm telling you now, you need to know. And you need to give a shit.

I'm not sure why most people would rather talk about anything other than retirement, but that seems to be the case. Perhaps thinking about retirement brings to mind thoughts of being grey haired and wrinkly. Perhaps it's the irrational belief that actually saving a large amount of money is impossible, which acts as a deterrent on even trying. Or perhaps people today are just ill-prepared to wait 30 years for a reward, as demonstrated by our willingness to pay extra money to skip levels in freemium games. Whatever the ultimate cause, we need to break free from it.

We need to start treating retirement accounts as sexy. And they are. What is sexier than retiring at a young age and being able to spend time traveling the world and spending more time with family and friends? Nothing. Your physical and mental health in the future is not worth buying a nicer car today.

Maybe we need to start making bumper stickers with catchy sayings like, "My other car is a 401K," or "Enjoy driving your luxury car to work when you're 80. I'll be on the beach."

Talk to anyone over 40 and they will all preach the same message, "I wish I started saving sooner." Why? Because small amounts saved at a young age can turn into huge sums later in life. Allow me to give you an example.

Instead of financing the purchase of a new car, you decide you will drive a slightly used car, bought with cash. You decide to start contributing what you would have paid monthly toward a car loan into a 401K. Using the average American's car payment of $415, saved monthly from ages 25-35, 10 years, in a 401K, and then left to grow for the next 30 years, you could retire at age 65 with about $600,000. Amazing, right? Your total contribution over that 10 year period would only have been $50,000.

So why is the average retirement savings for someone 65 in America only $49,000? Because when they were 25, they either didn't know about the power of compound interest or didn't care. Just as 25 year olds today don't care. START CARING. START SAVING.

Most companies have done away with pensions, viewing them as a long-term liability more than a way to retain top talent. Instead, they offer defined contribution plans that match the money you contribute to a retirement account, up to a set percentage. The problem with this is that you have to contribute to get the match. If you're not contributing and therefore not getting a match from your employer, you essentially have no retirement benefit from your company. Find out what your employer offers and get that match.

Still daydreaming about having a million dollars? Here is a simple breakdown from JP Morgan's 2014 "Guide to Retirement." Investing $6,000 a year, about $500 a month, from age 25-65 will bring you $1.1 million. Difficult, but manageable if you aren't loaded down with debt payments. If you wait until you are 35 to start saving, your required contribution climbs to $990 a month. Wait until 40 - brace yourself - almost $1,500 a month. It's suddenly starting to make sense why older individuals say they wish they started younger. Don't delay making contributions into a retirement account; you can't afford it.

Tip 18: So Many Choices...

You've landed your first job and know you need to set up your 401K. So, you dig into your company's offerings only to find yourself overwhelmed with choices. Mutual Funds, Index Funds, and Variable Annuity Funds (don't ever, ever, choose these). What is the difference and where the hell do you start?

There are two distinctly different ways to manage your retirement account: actively and passively. The active retirement account management style can be classified as someone who regularly checks their portfolio of stocks, bonds, etc., and makes changes to them. This can be done daily, weekly, or monthly. The passive investor on the other hand, maybe checks their retirement savings annually. The only adjustments they make are considered rebalancing, not actively managing.

I am going to talk specifically to the passive management style. Not only is this the most effective route for 90% of the population, it is also, in my personal opinion (and the scientific conclusion of multiple research papers) the method with the highest financial return.

The name of the game is "Fees." Your objective in this game is to minimize the fees your invested money is subjected to. What makes fees so detrimental to a retirement account is that they are charged whether you make money or lose money. Say you had an annual return on your retirement account of 6%. If you are paying 2.5% for a variable annuity fund, then your actual return that year was only 3.5%, not 6%. This is why Variable Annuities do not make sense for anyone contributing less than $18,000 annually to a 401K. That's not you? Good, stay away from variable annuities.

Did I mention you should stay away from Variable Annuities?

This leaves you with two choices: mutual funds and index funds. What's the difference? Mutual funds are actively managed. That means there is a team of people making decisions every day as to which stocks your retirement money should buy and sell. The idea being that these are "experts" who know what stocks will make money and which will lose money. Of course, you have to pay for "expertise." You can expect this expertise to cost you anywhere between 1% and 1.5% in fees.

Where do I put my money? Index funds. Low cost index funds only charge about 0.15% in fees. That's a lot less than the 2.5% annuity funds will cost you. How does this impact your total retirement fund over 30 years?

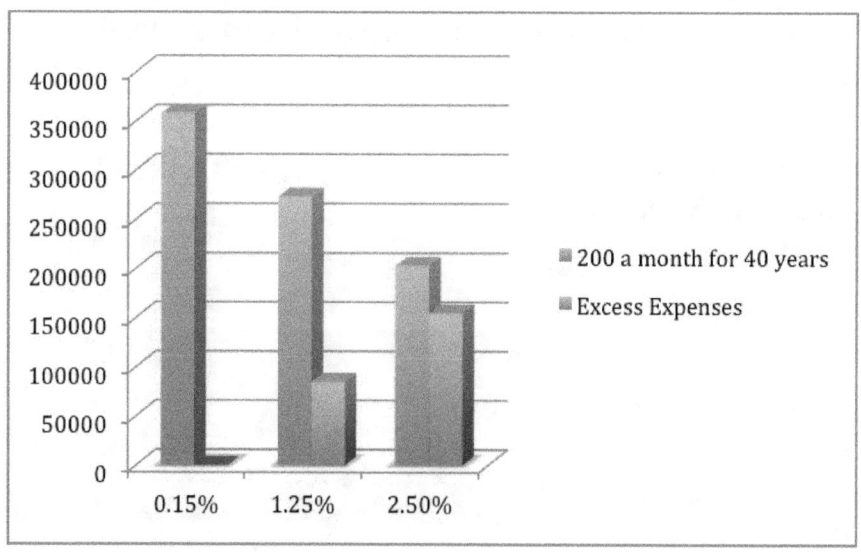

The above chart is based on a person contributing $200 a month from age 25 to age 65, earning a 6% average return, and paying the respective fees shown. As you can see, the index fund returns a significantly larger amount of money to the passive investor due simply to a lower fee structure. The difference between the fees paid by the index fund investor and the annuity fund investor is $154,000.

This is why you should avoid variable annuities like the plague, regardless of how well spoken and well dressed the commission-earning annuity pusher who came into your office or school is. And the term pusher is used intentionally here. Just as the drug dealer knows his product is detrimental to an individual's health, the annuity salesman, peddling his company's accounts to middle class workers, is equally aware of the destruction fees cause to retirement accounts.

How could he or she not be, when the Vice President of the National Association for Variable Annuities was quoted as saying variable annuities were only smart for individuals who "already maxed out their 401K and other qualified plans." Meaning, they're good for about 1% of the population. I think it's also safe to say if you're reading this book, you're not maxing out on your retirement contributions at the moment.

So, index funds minimize fees and as a result, boost an investor's lifetime return. Awesome. That still leaves you with a few hundred options.

At this point, it's really up to you. First, look at the different companies offering index funds. You want to look at how long they've been around, how highly the company is rated (which you can find at morningstar.com), and what fees their index funds are charging.

You should look to have a nice variety of index funds, encompassing both US and international stocks to be well diversified. If you don't want to diversify yourself, it gets even easier. Look for Lifecycle index funds. These funds come pre-diversified, if you will. All you have to do is pick the fund that closely aligns with your expected retirement date, and voila, it picks the risk strategy most appropriate for your age group. It will also rebalance for you, so you don't have to worry about making sure the percentage you allocated toward domestic stocks, international stocks, and so on, remain at those percentages.

Now, it is possible that your company could give you options consisting solely of mutual funds. That's OK. No need to panic. Figure out what your company will match for your contribution and ensure you get a full match. This is free money; do not miss out on it. If they match 3%, contribute 3% yourself to a mutual fund that attempts to closely track a large benchmark, such as the Dow Jones or S&P 500. These should also be some of the lowest fee mutual funds. This will put you at a 6% savings rate. You still need 4% more to hit that 10% target.

Set up a self-directed IRA (Individual Retirement Account), with a company that offers low cost index funds. Set up this 4% to be automatically distributed out of your paycheck to your new IRA. Pinky promising yourself that you'll do it each month will not cut it. Whatever company you choose to set up your account with will walk you through setting up your automatic contributions. Your HR department can also offer company-specific guidance on this, so be sure to check with them.

Remember, you are a passive investor. As a passive investor your number one objective is to minimize fees. Your number two objective is to minimize the amount of time you have to spend thinking about your retirement account. For the most hands-off, low-fee, approach to investing, look no further than Target Date index funds.

Tip 19: Net What? Net Worth

    Say you land a job making $200,000 a year. Awesome. With this salary you decide to buy a beautiful $550,000 home for your significant other and two children. You put down 10% and take a mortgage for $495,000. Such a beautiful home requires a set of equally magnificent cars to park in the garage. For you, it's the latest Range Rover for $75,000. Your spouse prefers a $55,000, ruby red, Mercedes convertible. You got both cars with 0% down and a 3% finance rate for 5 years. You and your spouse have $5,000 in the bank for a rainy day but have also racked up $9,000 in credit card debt. On top of all that, you still owe $80,000 on your student loans. Taken all together, this completes the "American Dream." What could possibly be so wrong about such a situation?

    If your children earn an allowance of, say, $20 a month, at the end of month one, your children have a **higher** net worth than **you**.

Net Worth - Children: $40

Net Worth - Parents: ($ 69,000)

Your children have $69,040 more than you do. Unbelievable as it may seem, all you have acquired in this hypothetical situation is debt. I used a large income to show that it doesn't matter if you earn a lot of money. People have an incredible way of matching their expenses directly to their income. Had the hypothetical You mentioned above earned $75,000 a year, bought a $200,000 home, and financed two cars, the outcome would remain the same. If your child found a penny on the floor, no one would have claim to that penny but them. If you found $10,000 on the floor, you'd be entitled to none of it.

If you have never taken the time to calculate your net worth, you should. It is a valuable exercise that shows you where you really stand. To do this, divide a sheet of paper in half. On one side, list your assets (what you have) against your liabilities (what you owe). To figure out what your cars are worth, use a website to find their current market value. The same goes for your house if you own one. Look up its current value on either Trulia or Zillow. The chart below is a sample I filled in with information from the hypothetical You in the scenario above. Take the time now to fill out your own balance sheet. We will wait for you to finish.

	Assets	Liabilities	Balance
Mortgage		($495,000)	

Car Loans		($130,000)	
Home	$550,000		
Cars	$90,000		
Student Loans		($80,000)	
Rainy Day Fund	$5,000		
Credit Cards		$9,000	
	$645,000	($714,000)	($69,000)

Hopefully, your number did not come out negative like our example. If it did, that's OK. The important thing is now you know. You cannot solve a problem you don't know exists.

Let's compare your net worth to the average American now. The average family with no college loans, according to a study done by Professor William Elliot III, has a net worth of $117,700. Obviously, this number encompasses individuals of all age groups. Don't be concerned if you're 30 with no college loans and don't yet have a net worth of $117,000. But it should definitely be a goal for 40. The average net worth for families with college debt drops dramatically to $42,800. That's a difference of almost $75,000.

While numerous studies have established that those with a college degree do earn a higher wage than those with only a high school diploma, those who had to take out loans to get their degree start their careers with a heavy burden to overcome.

So why should you care about your net worth if your salary currently supports your lifestyle on a month to month basis? Your net worth helps in determining when you can retire. Everyone's goal in life is to retire and live off of their assets. But most people have never taken five minutes to figure out what their assets are. The first time you figure out what your assets and liabilities are should not be when you're getting ready to retire. You need to track your net worth as you would track the stats of your favorite sports team. Learn what the budget cap for your team is, stay under it, cut expensive players if need be, and make sure the players you keep are worth what you're paying them.

Tip 20: Don't Fear the Stock Market

Fear the stock broker.

Several million people watched their retirement accounts shrivel in 2009, Mom and Dad included. It was horrific. If I had to compare it to a movie, I would choose *"House of a Thousand Corpses."* For those who haven't seen the movie, the title should give you a general idea of the plot. The crash was bad and retirement accounts were slaughtered.

Or at least that is how it seemed in the moment. Looking back on it now, the only people who lost money were the people who took their money out of the stock market as it crashed to the bottom. Anyone who left their money alone made all of their losses back, plus some extra. You may feel I am guilty of a "hindsight is 20/20" violation, but is it a violation if the hindsight I'm using has a 150 year history? The stock market has always regained its losses. Always.

It is not easy, while watching *"House of a Thousand Corpses,"* to imagine feeling safe in such a place. But what if you had already seen the movie? If you then found yourself at a shady house with some whacked out family, you would decline their dinner invitation and leave before they could make you corpse number one thousand and one. The stock market is nothing but a series of movie sequels that all share the same ending. In fact, it's a stereotypical suspense thriller. Everything is perfect - enter evil - everything turns to chaos - enter underdog hero - order is restored and everyone is surprised the hero pulled it off. But he always pulls it off.

2009 was the "everything turns to chaos" part. The evil was sub-prime lending. The technical jargon as to why it all happened is irrelevant. Just like the movies, they keep the same generic plot and just change the villain. Yet, no matter how many times we see the same story line, we always have that tinge of doubt in the back of our mind that maybe this movie is different. Maybe the bad guy will win this time. It's not. He won't.

Think of your retirement account as a rope. This rope is attached at one end to a winch, over which you have no control. The winch is automated, retracting the rope in and letting it out at random intervals and at different lengths each time. At the other end of this rope is you. As the winch releases or retracts the rope, you either ascend or descend inside a pit filled with snakes. This equates to the movement of your retirement account within the stock market.

In 2008, the winch had pulled people so high up in the pit that they forgot about the snakes at the bottom. They were so high they could no longer hear the hissing. It seemed like the winch would forever pull them higher. Then, in 2009, the winch began releasing the slack very quickly. As people descended into the pit, they began to hear the hissing of the snakes below. This was a noise they had grown unaccustomed to. It made their pulse race, their palms sweat, their nights sleepless. As the fear that they may soon reach the snakes grew, some began clinging to the wall and cutting their ropes. The darkness obscured the true depth of the pit so no one could tell where the bottom truly was.

These rope cutters are the individuals who sold their stocks while the market was at its lowest point. In their state of panic they decided it would be safer and easier to climb back up on their own. This idea was reinforced as they watched the rope descend even further from the point they had freed themselves. Until something incredible happened, the winch started pulling the rope back up. It started slowly at first, but then in 2013 the rope shot up toward the top of the pit. Those who cut the rope in 2009 were trapped at the bottom of the well unable to grasp the rope that had risen beyond their reach.

The wall climbers are now left to grab onto a new rope. This one was dropped down to the low part of the well where they are, but it is attached to the same winch. It is unlikely that the winch will pull them up as far as it did the others last year. To the contrary, it is much more likely to raise them up only a little before it starts lowering them again. If they had only hung onto the first rope, they'd be back at the top of the well.

My pit and rope analogy can be dragged out infinitely. Diversification, for example can be represented by multiple ropes, each attached to its own winch. The idea being that all the winches won't lower you into the pit of snakes at the same time. Account fees can be thought of as a missing tooth on the main gear of the winch. Every time you go a full rotation, either up or down, you fall down a notch as the motor slips past the missing tooth. If you earned money, you fall a notch. If you lost money, you fall an additional notch. The fact that fees hurt you in good times and bad is why your ultimate goal is to minimize your fees. Sure there are people who will try to sell you a motor with multiple missing teeth, ensuring you that it's OK if you fall two notches every rotation because this winch goes up more often than down. But the truth is they don't know. So the brokers are in no position to testify to the quality of one winch over the next. They take educated guesses at best, follow hunches at worst. One thing is for certain: if you're investing in a fund with high investment fees, you're buying a winch that falls two notches every year.

Tip 21: Retire Debt Free

I have gone to great lengths to demonstrate how we are brought up in a debt-loving culture. While this is costly and imprudent while young, it can be even more devastating as you approach retirement. Every percent interest you are paying towards a debt is a percent being eaten from your retirement account.

The average retirement account has a balance of $49,000. Assuming you're earning a 6% average annual return on a balanced retirement plan, you make about $2,940 in interest annually. Not a bad sum. If we also factor in your investment account being a mutual fund, we have to consider the management fee they charge annually, somewhere in the ballpark of 1.25%. This reduced the interest earned on the year by $615, bringing the total down to $2,327.50.

Now, let us add in the average amount of estimated debt that Americans carry. The average family's credit card debt is $8,800, with an interest rate of 15%. The interest that would be charged on that debt is $1,320. This would reduce your yearly earned retirement interest to $1,007.50. In just two simple steps we've reduced your estimated yearly interest earned by almost two-thirds. Who cares if your retirement account is earning $3,000 a year if you only get to keep $1,000 of it?

No one is in an uproar about this situation because the eroding of your wealth is happening below the surface. If you want to know the management fee of your mutual fund or other retirement account, you're going to have a hell of a time finding it. I recently searched through my wife's retirement account to find their fee structure. It took me 30 minutes to find it. Most people would have probably given up before then and that is what the company is banking on. Similarly, credit card companies don't want you to spend time thinking about how much interest you have paid this year or how much you paid last year. They just tack the interest on to your existing balance, hidden right in there with your current purchases. You never have to see it, never have to think about it. And they think that is just fine.

Your goal in retirement is to have a lot of assets and very little liabilities. If you are carrying credit card and personal loan debt, you are saddling yourself with the worst possible liabilities. These two forms of debt carry the highest interest rates and can quickly eat away at any interest you are earning on investments.

People generally don't think about interest they pay on their debts as being a counterweight to interest they earn on assets. Even the pros make this simple mistake. While watching a daily CNBC broadcast, one male anchor described his "portfolio" of stocks as having gained 12% in interest this year. A portfolio is a collection of any variety of investments pooled together that represents an investor's strategy. He was very proud of his 12% return, as he should be. But then, a new guest came on the show from Chase Bank. During his interview, that same male host stated that he loves his Chase credit card and that it is "generally maxed out."

As I sighed to myself over how socially acceptable it is to brag about being maxed out on any form of credit, I thought back to this anchor's 12% portfolio return he claimed to have made. How would that 12% look if he added the negative interest his maxed out credit card is earning? Probably not as rosy.

The other side of this coin is that credit card interest rates stay the same, while portfolio returns can vary widely, even turning negative. If this CNBC host's portfolio gains 12% but he's paying 20% interest on his maxed out credit card, his true total return might only be 9%. Worse yet, if his portfolio has a bad year and loses money, say negative 4%, then he loses another 20% on his credit card debt, his total losses could be increased to 7 or 8%. The only thing credit card debt can do is lower your retirement returns in good years and exacerbate your losses in bad years.

Your Receipt

1.   Start saving for retirement *now*.

2. $415 per month saved between ages 25 -
35, invested for 30 years, would be $600,000
at age 65.

3.   Investing $500 a month from age 25 - 65
will make you a millionaire.

4.   Net worth is Assets minus Liabilities (debts).

5.   The stock market is still the best way for you
to build wealth and save for retirement.

Get rid of all of your debt before retirement or it will
erode your hard earned savings.

Chapter 5:
70/20/10 Rule

How It Works

I mention the 70/20/10 rule in two different chapters in this book, and for good reason. If you adopt the 70/20/10 rule in your life, you will become debt free and you will have a healthy retirement savings. Here is how this simple rule accomplishes all of that.

Save 10%

If you save 10% of your salary each year, in ten years how much will you have saved? The equivalent of a whole year's salary. If you make $50,000 a year, you will have saved $50,000. That is impressive when you consider the average retirement savings in America is only $49,000. While this may seem like an impossible task, you can make it easy. Make it automatic.

Through the magic of direct deposit, you can have 10% of your pay directly diverted into a retirement or savings account without it ever reaching your checking account. If you never see the money, you can't spend it. If it seems hard at first to jump to 10% from 0%, you can make the change gradually. Start at 1% and slowly raise the percentage to 10% at a pre-set interval.

The key here is that you set an interval and stick to it. Will you raise your percentage every month, once a quarter, or every six months? Whatever you choose, hold yourself to it. Put it on the calendar, set a reminder on your phone, set an event date on Facebook, or do all three. The key is that you stick with it and bump your contribution up to 10%. Once you're there, any raise that you receive at work will also result in an increase in your monthly savings. It all becomes automatic and automatic is as easy as it gets.

Some of you may work for employers who can set you up with an automatic contribution increase. If this is the case, your goal of 10% savings becomes even easier to achieve. At a predetermined interval, your company will automatically raise your 401K contribution 1% until you hit the maximum contribution you have set for yourself.

Debt Payments 20%

You have to get rid of your debts. The money you spend on interest is money that just evaporates from your pocket. Think of it as a tax on impatience. If you had waited until you had enough money to purchase the item you wanted, you would not have to pay any interest. But because you had to buy that item right now, you're incurring a 22% impatience tax every month you don't pay it off in full.

Use 20% of your income to get rid of your impatience tax penalties.

What if your debt payments each month are greater than 20% of your income? Call your lenders and try to negotiate your payments down or work toward having your interest rate cut. Explain to them the situation you are now in. You owe more each month than you can afford to pay. These companies are in the business of making money. If you go broke and can't pay them at all anymore, they don't make money.

Most companies will be willing to work with you. Even at a reduced interest rate, these companies are still making a ton of money off of you. Of course, once you've done this, you need to **stop using credit**. You cannot pay down debt if you are still continually adding to it. That would be like trying to drain a bathtub with the faucet still on. Pick one credit card to keep in case of emergencies.

An emergency is defined as your car breaking down on the highway and needing to be towed, your furnace died at 2 a.m. and it's 10 degrees outside, or some other instance out of your control that **needs** to be fixed for you to remain **safe** and **healthy**. No other condition that does not immediately impact your safety or well-being constitutes an emergency.

Once you've been building your savings for a while, you will no longer have an emergency require a credit card to cover the payment. At that point you will be free from the revolving credit trap you've been stuck in for so long.

Spend 70%

You do not have to live like a hermit to build wealth. You should enjoy spending most of the money you make. After all, you worked hard for it. The hard part is only spending 70% of your pay.

This does not mean spend 70% and then make up for any shortfalls with your credit card. This means only spend 70%.

If you're looking at your monthly expenses on a spreadsheet and thinking to yourself, I cannot live on 70% of my income, then you have just taken a giant leap in the right direction. If you cannot live on 70%, you're living wrong.

Fortunately, you found this book, and now you know what needs to change. Not only do you know what needs to change, but you now have the tools in your financial toolbox to change it. Take out your shiny new financial chisel and start chipping away at the monthly expenses that are bleeding you dry.

Perhaps you need to get out of your car lease. Or maybe you have the premium, ultra, cable package, and you could reduce what you subscribe to. Only you, looking at your specific financial situation can identify the areas that you are simply spending too much on.

If you're having a hard time cutting a specific something out of your budget, think about what its total yearly cost is. Then decide if you think it would be worth it if you had to pay cash, up front, every year for this service. Would you do it? If not, chisel it away.

The Reward

After all of this financial sacrifice, you must be thinking to yourself, does it ever get better? Can I ever enjoy more of my money? And the answer is YES.

After you have paid off all of your debts, you will suddenly find yourself with a 20% raise. No longer having to pay impatience tax, you will have 20% more each month to spend how you wish.

Do whatever you want with it.

You can save this money for a family vacation. You could save and buy the new tech gadget you have put off buying while you eliminated your debt. You worked hard, you deserve a reward.

Of course, I do have a recommendation. Switch to an 85/15 split between your spending and saving. Giving your savings that extra 5% bump will ensure a comfortable retirement under most circumstances in the future. You are free to go to a full 90/10 split if you choose; 10% is still excellent. But if you have been living on 70%, jumping up to 85% will still feel pretty darn good.

Happy Saving

Your Receipt

1.   Saving 10% of your income does two things: it gets you in the habit of saving and it provides a safety net if an emergency comes up.

2.   Having savings to dip into can prevent you from taking on additional high-interest debt.

3.   Pay down debt systematically. Once a debt is paid off, roll that payment to the next debt on your hit list.

4.   Learn to live on 70% of your income. If you're spending more than 70% of your income each month on living expenses start cutting – dinners out, premium cable bills, expensive to maintain toys, etc.

Once your debts are paid off, you can put that "extra" money towards living expenses, savings, or some combination of both.

Chapter 6:

Being the Third Pig

Bonus Tip: Imagine Your Future

I hope it is becoming clear by now that the foundation we are building our futures on, that we have been told to build our futures on, is poorly constructed. Debt is sold to us as the cheapest and fastest way to build our house of dreams. What they don't tell us in the sales pitch is that this foundation cannot weather even the lightest storm.

One tale that we are all familiar with is the *Three Little Pigs*. Mom and Dad would read this story each night as they sought to teach us the lessons of hard work and patience. Spend some extra time on things that matter and you will not get eaten by the Wolf. These same lessons can be expanded to include your finances.

Think of the first and second pig as the ones who buy everything on credit. Their cars are leased. They refinance their homes after paying down the principal for only a few years. They have all the latest technology and probably an amazing kitchen. Sure, they have seen the Wolf come and blow down other people's homes. But their situation is different. Their job is secure. As long as they can keep making all the monthly payments on time, they can keep the Wolf at bay.

What we know for sure is bad things happen to good people. People get hurt, jobs get downsized, life happens. If the life around you is built on credit, then your home is built with sticks and straw. Should the Wolf of misfortune choose to visit you, the weakness of your structure will become much more apparent. When the jowls of the finance companies are chomping at your door day and night, you will not find peace wherever you go. When you realize that the well-being and future of your family is protected solely by stick and straw walls, a new perspective will emerge.

Do I need the nicest car? Does it matter what stove is in my kitchen if the one I have feeds my family just fine? Do I need a 50 inch TV in every room and a thousand cable channels? If the choice in your life is between any of these items and groceries, the answer suddenly becomes easy.

My Dad drove the two worst cars I've ever seen in my life for a few years after he lost his job. Did it matter what people thought of him, driving around in those go-carts with doors? Nope, he was taking care of his family. The sad part was watching my family have to survive living life as the first two pigs in the story. Our house of straw was blown down when the Wolf stopped by. It took every ounce of effort my Mom and Dad had to make sure it did not affect my brother and me at all.

Our lifestyles had to change. The house got smaller and the cars more economical. The lesson I learned from all of this: it didn't matter how big our house was, if we drove Camaros or purple Hyundai Accents. We were happy because we were together and we were healthy. Everything else in life was just noise.

The fact remains however, that if we had built our lives like the third pig, maybe the Wolf would have been unable to shake our foundation the way he did.

I don't want each and every one of my peers to have to learn financial lessons the hard way. Listening to stories of students graduating with hundreds of thousands of dollars of student loan debt, then taking on multiple credit cards, racking up more debt, only to be sold high-fee retirement accounts is heartbreaking.

It seems all so trivial now, with so many years ahead of us before retirement. But the reality is so much of what your future will become is being paved right now. Your ability to contribute to a retirement account starting at a young age will be the determining factor of how much free money you will be able to spend when you get older. The older you are when you start saving for retirement, the more money each month you have to contribute to get the same return. Wait too long, and catching up becomes an impossibility.

Taking on massive amounts of consumer debt is the fastest way to destroy a healthy retirement before it ever starts.

With these tips, you can begin to build a new life for yourself. One filled with less stress, less debt, and more wealth. You now know how to distinguish between actual wealth and the illusion of wealth. How to avoid the scams that seek to separate you from your hard-earned money. You should never again look at finance offers as opportunities to get what you want but as traps to keep you from achieving the financial independence that you need. We have stepped outside the box to look back in and I hope what you learned upset you. I hope it made you angry. I know when I was learning everything I know now, and everything I continue to learn, every new piece of information made me angrier than the last.

This is good. This anger can be turned into passion for change. It drove me to take a hard look at the way I handle my money. When I did, I realized that whenever financial pundits on TV were talking about "the consumer" they were referring to me. We are all debt consumers. We are not the customers as much as we are the product. Companies offering you credit, offer you up in return to their shareholders as a user with an appetite for debt. You are sold as a commodity. The difference between the commodities you buy and the people who buy shares of you is the people buying you are paying cash.

Be the third pig.

Build your financial foundation with patience and effort like the third pig using your new Debt Free Mind.

Your Receipt

1. Have a rainy-day fund.

    a. At a minimum, 3 months of living

        expenses (6 is preferable).

    b. As your monthly liabilities grow, so

        must your fund.

    c. Build up your fund in anticipation of

        new liabilities, not after you acquire them.

2. Do not carry credit card balances.

3. Do not lease your vehicles.

    a. If you run into financial trouble, you can't

    even sell it. They just take it away and you are

    left with nothing. You also are setting yourself

    up to have a car payment forever. Literally until

    you die.

4. Minimize college loans any way possible.

   a. Paying down the loans while still in school is an excellent way to do this.

   b. Avoid private loans. Stay Federal.

   c. Remember, it's real money. It's your money.

5. Do not use store financing for purchases.

6. Buy slightly used, refurbished, or ding & dent stores items if you absolutely need them but don't have a lot of money.

   a. A new couch is only different from the floor model in the store until you whack it the first time with the vacuum.

7. Save at least 10% of your income for retirement, TODAY.

8. Find out if your company offers a 401(k) with contribution match.

   a. Get that match. It's free money.

9. Watch out for Small Number Shenanigans,

it's everywhere.

10.   Learn to take pride in your financial

security more than in your possessions.

Want more from the Debt Free Mind?

Visit

WWW.THEDEBTFREEMIND.COM

Where you'll find free templates to help you manage your money.

Subscribe and receive my free eBook

Be sure to keep and eye out for my upcoming book:

The Debt-Zombie Survival Guide